BROOKE'S
BATTERY
PHILIP SPINKS

Lord Brooke with a 15 Pounder gun. His young attendant is believed to be his son.
(Photo: WCRO CR 1886 / Box 790.)

BROOKE'S
BATTERY
PHILIP SPINKS

A History of

1/1 WARWICKSHIRE ROYAL HORSE ARTILLERY
1908 ~ 1919

BREWIN BOOKS

First published by
Brewin Books Ltd, 56 Alcester Road,
Studley, Warwickshire B80 7LG in 2008
www.brewinbooks.com

ISBN: 978-1-85858-422-5

A Cataloguing in Publication Record
for this title is available from the British Library.

Typeset in Bembo
Printed in Great Britain by
The Alden Press.

CONTENTS

ACKNOWLEDGEMENTS

The author is not a military historian; it is fair to say that this book is as much a local history as a military one. Therefore, I would like to extend my thanks to the following for enlightening me on many aspects of the history of the Warwickshire Royal Horse Artillery and the Royal Regiment of Artillery: Lieutenant Colonel W Townend MA of the Royal Artillery Historical Society; Mr Bryan Owen of Leamington Spa (who kindly provided much detail for the Appendices); and Mr Michael Caldwell of Stratford-upon-Avon.

I would also wish to thank the following for their valuable assistance: Mr C Towner, Editor of the Stratford-upon-Avon Herald; Mr M Lawson, Editor of the Leamington Spa Courier; Mr Garen Ewing of East Grinstead; Mr Tony Smith of Lyme Regis; the staff at Shakespeare Birthplace Trust Records Office, Stratford-upon-Avon; the staff at Warwick County Record Office; and the staff at Leamington Spa Public Library.

I have been unable to locate some copyright holders, but would welcome them to contact me.

A NOTE ON RANKS

The following ranks were used for Royal Artillery junior non-commissioned officers prior to 1920: Bombardier [Lance Bombardier post 1920] and Corporal [Bombardier post 1920], ranks which correspond with Lance Corporal and Corporal in most other units of the army.

ABOUT THE AUTHOR

Philip Spinks is a native of Stratford-upon-Avon. He served with the Royal Artillery and the Sultan of Oman's Artillery. He now works as an ambulance paramedic. Among his hobbies is local history and he is a volunteer at the Shakespeare Birthplace Trust Records Office. He is married with one son.

INTRODUCTION

1/1 Warwickshire Royal Horse Artillery was raised in 1908 as a unit in the newly established Territorial Force and was disbanded in 1919. The Battery was composed of volunteer soldiers from all walks of life recruited from Warwickshire and was the first Territorial artillery unit to go to France in the First World War.

The Battery's peacetime training was carried out mostly in-house and under financial constraints; nevertheless a fine team spirit quickly developed which was to stand the Battery in good stead in August 1914.

The Battery's war service was exemplary; whether firing their guns in support of the cavalry or the infantry the men rose to all challenges they met. The conditions in which the men served were mostly appalling; it has been suggested that only twice since the First World War – at the battles of Monte Cassino and Stalingrad – have soldiers suffered so much. But the men of 1/1 Warwickshire Royal Horse Artillery faced the atrocious conditions and dangerous situations in which they found themselves with fortitude, endurance, courage and humour. They may have travelled to France as 'amateurs', but they soon became as professional as their regular counterparts. And they always found time for a game of football!

The Battery's war service can be broken into two parts; from late-1914 until late-1916 it was attached to cavalry divisions and saw comparatively little action, after late-1916 and until the end of the war it was supporting infantry and had little rest from intense activity.

This little book presents the story of this almost forgotten artillery battery that played a small part in mankind's first industrialised war: a war few of the volunteers would have anticipated and in which fewer still would have expected to have been engaged. The Battery earned its fair share of gallantry awards but, unfortunately, a large proportion of Battery members did not return home at war's end.

Field Marshal Montgomery wrote, in 1955, that he knew '... the Warwickshire soldier well... they never failed to do what was asked of them and they always did it very well.' Montgomery was alluding to Warwickshire infantrymen at the time; he may as well have been describing those volunteers who served the guns with 1/1 Warwickshire Royal Horse Artillery.

Chapter One

FORMATION AND TRAINING

In December 1905 Richard Burdon Haldane[1] became Secretary of State for War in Sir Henry Campbell Bannerman's newly elected Liberal government. Haldane was to remain at the War Office until 1912 and during his time there he completed a thorough and revolutionary transformation of the British Army. Haldane had been deeply concerned about the British Army's performance during the Boer War; as early as 1901 he had wanted a '... comparatively small Army... one extremely efficacious and capable for foreign service.' By early-1906 Haldane had set about a re-organisation of the British Army and plans were drawn up to produce an expeditionary force capable of fighting a European war – probably against Germany. This re-organisation of the Army was carried out in a period of retrenchment; even within the financial constraints though, Haldane's scheme was a success and once complete an army had been formed which, by late-1914 '... worked more efficiently than any other British army at the start of a major war.' (The War Secretary's achievement had been timely: recent research has shown that Germany was planning, as early as 1907, an invasion of Britain.)[2]

Haldane was equally keen to reform the non-professional army too: the yeomanry, volunteers and militia – local, county based units – would become, Haldane opined: '... a real national army, formed by the people... It might be styled the Territorial Army.' (This people's army was actually called the Territorial Force (TF) until 1921, when Territorial Army was adopted.) The responsibility for running this new home army would be passed to Territorial Force Associations – fourteen for the entire country – with directions from the Army Council.

---

[1] For full biographical details of Haldane see *Oxford Dictionary of National Biography* Oxford, 2004 vol 24, pp.513–23.

[2] See David Keys 'How the First World War was predicted' *BBC History* vol 7, no 1, January 2006 p.6.

Warwickshire, which then included Coventry and Birmingham, had its own Association. Such a force, fully trained and equipped and ready to augment the regular army would, Haldane thought, negate the need for conscription in the event of war. The Territorial Force would be used for homeland defence only and would only be committed to overseas service on a voluntary basis.

The Territorial Force would, for the first time, see the Yeomanry regiments supported by dedicated horse artillery.[3] The new Royal Horse Artillery batteries would be raised in twelve counties: Hampshire, Essex, Glamorgan, Ayrshire, Inverness-shire, Shropshire, West Riding [of Yorkshire], Somerset, Warwickshire, Berkshire, Leicestershire and Nottinghamshire.

In late-1907 and early-1908 the Warwickshire Territorial Association, based in offices in High Street, Warwick, debated the issue of raising a battery of Royal Horse Artillery (RHA) within the county. The early meetings of the Association were convened by the Marquess of Hertford (the Lord Lieutenant of Warwickshire and President of the Association) with Sir Henry Fairfax-Lucy as Chairman. The Association comprised aristocracy, retired Army officers and local politicians including the Lord Mayor of Birmingham, the Mayor of Coventry and a Birmingham industrialist with an eye to a political future, Neville Chamberlain. All were keen to see the formation of a Warwickshire Royal Horse Artillery battery and plans were made to do so. (Although there was an input from Birmingham representatives to the Association, there would be no Birmingham men in the battery when it formed.)

The early months of 1908 saw a countywide recruiting campaign for men to join the new unit. This campaign was not an easy one. The Marquess of Hertford, at a meeting in London on 26 November 1908, spoke of the pressure that had been placed upon Warwickshire ('... not a very big county...') to provide the Territorial Force units required of it in addition to the RHA battery: '... a regiment of Yeomanry, four battalions of infantry, three batteries of field artillery, a battery of garrison artillery, two howitzer batteries, two companies of transport, three companies of engineers, and two ambulances, besides an ambulance mounted brigade.'[4] Most of the Territorial units within Warwickshire had been

---

3   The Royal Horse Artillery (RHA) gave close artillery support to cavalry units; the Royal Field Artillery (RFA) did the same for infantry units.

4   *Stratford-upon-Avon Herald* 4 December 1908 p.2.

re-organised or re-formed from previously existing cadres, but the requirements were still great before the inception of horse artillery. The formation of an entirely new unit would be onerous and the full establishment of the battery was announced in January 1908 at a meeting of the Territorial Association: '... a horse artillery battery ... an Ammunition Column, 7 officers, 317 men.'[5] The manning figures were based on a battery of six guns, but a short while later it was decided that the battery would field four guns only and therefore the manning requirement was reduced to 7 officers and 214 NCOs and men.

The first Battery Commander of Warwickshire Royal Horse Artillery was to be Lord Brooke, the son and heir of the Earl of Warwick, in the rank of major.[6] At the time Brooke was *aide-de-camp* to Sir John French and leave of absence had to be gained from his superior before Brooke could take up his post. French gave his permission on the condition that Brooke raised '... a battery which shall be a model to the whole Territorial Army.'[7] Brooke promised to do so. Regular soldiers were appointed to the embryonic battery to provide professional advice and experience and to run the battery on a day-to-day basis: an Adjutant, Captain WAS Gemmell formerly of 'Z' Battery Royal Horse Artillery and a veteran of the Boer War and Sergeant Major Freddie Waters who was assisted by at least one NCO, Corporal Thompson.

A temporary headquarters was made available at Warwick Castle where the stable block would house the horses, guns and equipment (although large and solidly built with a good central courtyard, it would have been unable to accommodate all the horses of a battery)[8] and the Shakespeare Room, within the

---

5   *Warwick and Warwickshire Advertiser and Leamington Gazette* 11 January 1908 p.6.
6   Leopold Guy Francis Greville, Lord Brooke (1882–1928) was a military man. He had absconded from Eton and sold some of his possessions to afford his way to South Africa in 1899 to take part in the Boer War. He was immediately taken on the staff of Sir John French, then a cavalry commander of some renown, and was commissioned into 1st Life Guards in 1900, and saw active service there. He covered the Russo-Japanese War for Reuters and later worked for the *Morning Post* in Macedonia and Serbia.
7   *Warwick Advertiser* 4 February 1928 p.6, quoting Lord French from a eulogy he made to Brooke after the latter's death. Lords Brooke and French had been very close friends since the General had taken Brooke 'under his wing' as a young 'school leaver'.
8   Horses were a problem for Territorial Force artillery units. When not on annual camp, when military horses would be supplied for the duration, a very small number were on battery strengths. The grooming and welfare of the horses was done by the permanent staff and any volunteers who were able to assist. The number of horses for full detachments of a four gun battery of 12 Pounders was 72. The horses for the officers, the Ammunition Column (always under strength during peacetime), and others would have raised the total horses required to well over 120.

castle, would provide office and stores accommodation. Lea Fields, part of the castle estate, would be used as a drilling ground. Of all the new Royal Horse Artillery batteries, unquestionably Warwickshire's had the most prestigious address in the country! At first sight the provision of Warwick Castle as a headquarters for the new battery would seem a good example of *noblesse oblige* on the part of Lord Brooke or his father, the earl. But rent was demanded as was due to those providing accommodation for Territorial Force units *via* the county Association to the tune of £100 *per annum*. Gemmell assiduously chased the Association for each quarterly payment on behalf of the Battery Commander/'landlord'. And the use of the stable block for a Territorial Force unit allowed the hot water system there to be repaired; the invoice being sent to the Territorial Association for payment.[9]

With the headquarters established, a recruitment drive began in earnest. The personnel of an artillery battery at that time (as now) required many skills, not least the ability to ride: no motor transport was available; everything depended on horse power. As well as gunners and drivers there was a need for farriers, shoeing smiths, fitters, saddlers, wheelwrights, cooks, storemen and clerks. Some of these trades could be learned as part of the volunteers' training but some were specialist. A battery had to be self-contained and self-administered. It was hoped that the north of the county would supply skilled, mechanically minded men due to the engineering and industrial base thereabouts and that the mainly agricultural south would provide men who knew about horses, although this, of course, was not exclusive. This rationale, although simplistic, was reasonable but it must be assumed that some of the volunteers would have neither technical nor horsemanship skills.

The local press published reports of the foundation of the Battery and supported the recruitment campaign. Predicting a successful raising of the Battery, the *Stratford-upon-Avon Herald* declared:

In this incipient stage of the battery, four fifteen pound [*sic*] guns have been converted into quick firers, and this really looks like business. Any young and

---

9 Warwick County Record Office (WCRO) CR 1886/Box 959. Also included is a letter, dated 23 January 1909, from Lord Brooke to his father which alludes to the possible use of St John's House, Warwick as a headquarters for the higher rent of £150 *per annum*. The more spacious accommodation there would allow the soldiers to have a social club for which they could pay 1/– *per* month. This plan did not come to fruition.

patriotic fellow requiring information [should apply to] the temporary headquarters of the force at Warwick Castle.[10]

The news that four guns were available, however, was erroneous: Warwickshire RHA was not to receive its complement of guns for some time. The same newspaper also carried a large advertisement for recruits.[11]

Public meetings were held throughout the county to encourage would-be volunteers to come forward to join the Battery. One such meeting, held at the White Swan public house in Henley in Arden, was called by Mr Couchman, the town's high bailiff. He had not only managed to gather local dignitaries but also the Earl of Warwick who attended to support Lord Brooke. Also present was the Battery Sergeant Major, Freddie Waters. The earl spoke at length and admitted his Conservatism and his dislike for change, but endorsed Haldane's reforms and explained that although Warwickshire had its units of Volunteers and Yeomanry, no one actually knew what their role would be in the event of war. The earl reinforced the idea of a Territorial Force being a homeland defence force, one '... designed to protect their hearths and homes, their wives and families, if they were called upon...'

Lord Brooke then addressed the meeting and gave information about the Battery's organisation and the pay and conditions for recruits to the Battery. He wanted the Warwickshire RHA to be the 'best battery in England.' He explained that enlistment would be for four years (with the horse artillery getting slightly better pay and increased allowances than the Yeomanry due to extra riding and driving practice and that the drills were harder than for the cavalry); that 214 men (154 for the guns and 60 for the Ammunition Column) and 7 officers were required; that annual grants would be £5 *per* horse, plus £1 equitation grant, if recruits supplied their own mounts; that whilst on annual camp of sixteen days *per* year each man would receive 4/d per day and allowances. 'This new battery would become so efficient as to inspire the Yeomanry with the same feeling of confidence that the regular forces had in the Royal Horse Artillery', predicted Brooke.[12]

---

[10] *Herald* 20 March 1908 p.8.
[11] *Herald* 1 May 1908 p.4.
[12] *Herald* 15 May 1908 p.3.

And to strengthen the recruitment campaign, in late–May 1908 Lord Brooke and Captain Gemmell rode through the streets of Stratford–upon–Avon followed by a fully crewed gun drawn by six horses.[13] (This must have been a crew from an established battery as Warwickshire RHA had yet to receive its guns.) This would not have been an isolated incident; although no other reports have been found it is highly likely that Brooke, Gemmell and gun team drove through most of the county's towns. Lord Brooke led the recruitment campaign personally and with much vigour: he considered the Battery his own property and he was under an obligation to French. Brooke was ably supported by his regular staff; without them his would have been a lost cause. But very soon his efforts had borne fruit. A rapid influx of recruits had joined Warwickshire RHA and by mid–June 1908 the Army Council recognised the Battery as a unit of the Territorial Force as it had achieved 30% of its manning. This was no mean feat when the county's other Territorial Force recruitment drives were under way at the same time.

In the following month figures were published which showed that the county Territorial Force establishment stood at 159 officers and 4589 Other Ranks (68% and 65% respectively of the required numbers). The Yeomanry was fullest manned, the Ambulance the least. Warwickshire RHA had by then 135 recruits – or 63% of its establishment figure.[14] It is difficult to say what inspired the recruits to fill the ranks of the new battery. Local newspapers made much of a man's patriotic duty to fulfil the requirements for home defence and few would have been unaware of the threat posed by Germany (although this threat would have seemed much less than in the late–1930s). Part time soldiering would have appealed to those with a wish for such activity and the chance to work closely with the Warwickshire Yeomanry – seen by many within the Warwickshire population as the cream of the local Territorial Force – would have carried a certain cachet; some were ex-servicemen, possibly hankering after the *esprit de corps* and comradeship of a military unit; the additional income would have appealed to some; while the chance to travel to annual camp (at a time when working class men had little chance to travel

---

[13] *Herald* 5 June 1908 p.5.

[14] *Warwick Advertiser* 4 July 1908 p.5. It will be seen that overall, Warwickshire RHA's percentage manning was below average, but their numbers had risen by 33% after being recognised by the Army Council.

anywhere, even within their own country) would have been seen by some as a definite perk; perhaps some had been unable to join the Yeomanry but thought their horsemanship could be employed. A structured ranking system and the appointment of NCOs shortly after the formation of the Battery indicates that some of the volunteers were ex-military and brought with them experience.

It is worth mentioning here that the recruitment of officers was somewhat problematic. By Spring 1910, only three officers (of the Battery's establishment of seven) were in place. Even as late as 1914 a local aristocrat, Lord Willoughby de Broke of Compton Verney near Kineton, was most forthright in his condemnation of the lack of response from men of 'the comfortable and privileged classes' in joining the Territorial Force. Tabling an amendment to the Territorial Forces Act in January 1914 he opined that '... property and privilege could only be honourably enjoyed if it were accompanied by the discharge of duty... the essential points of [this amendment are] that the comfortable classes should be forced to serve, the poorer classes would be invited to enlist on a voluntary basis.'[15] Willoughby de Broke's annoyance did not apply to Warwickshire RHA at that time, since in 1911 the Earl of Clonmel (a Liberal firebrand from Princethorpe, near Rugby) and in 1913 Lord Poulett (an ex-Second Lieutenant in the Highland Light Infantry) had joined the Battery Ammunition Column as officers.

The first few months of 1908 would have been a trying time for all involved with Warwickshire RHA, but the permanent staff must have felt particularly strained: not only did they have to recruit personnel but they had to form an entire battery from scratch. Administration, organisation, training, equipment and uniform ordering, receipt and issue all fell to them. Theirs was an unenviable task, but one which was performed well and efficiently as 'The battery recently formed by Lord Brooke is making splendid progress. The men are evidently very proud of their battery, and the county will have reason to be proud of them when they become, as they will in time, one of the best batteries of horse artillery in the territorial army.'[16]

---

[15]　*Warwick Advertiser* 31 January 1914 p.6.

[16]　*Warwick Advertiser* 19 July 1908 p.5. There is little doubt that this report in the local press was instigated by Brooke himself.

The Battery was subjected to various inspections by military dignitaries during its formation. The first formal inspection was carried out by the Marquess of Hertford at Warwick Castle on 10 October 1908. At the inspection the marquess had admitted to being sceptical about raising a horse artillery battery and that his scepticism had been shared by other experienced artillery officers. Such scepticism was thwarted by what he saw at the inspection which was a great success, even if there were no horses! The three guns – one 15 Pounder and two 12 Pounders – had to be manhandled into and out of action by the crews who had lain down '... imaginary fire upon an imaginary enemy.'[17] The Battery had indeed come some way in less than ten months.

Any frustration felt by the lack of equipment and horses could not be blamed upon anyone within the Battery. It is obvious that for all the hopes, plans and promises of Whitehall the actual 'nuts and bolts' for the new units, or at least Warwickshire RHA, were not forthcoming. By the end of 1908 the Battery had three guns (not four) of two types, all quickly approaching obsolescence. They did not have sufficient horses to pull their under-gunned battery or its wagons. But what they did have was an enthusiasm for 'Saturday night soldiering'.

Training programmes were conscientiously adhered to. Although recruits had come from all parts of Warwickshire, the training was centred on the Warwick and Leamington Spa areas. The dedication of these men to travel across the county to attend training must be acknowledged (as should the public transport system of the time!). Training took place every night from Monday to Friday and on Saturday afternoons, giving the men a chance to attend at least once a week. As an example, the third week of December 1908 began on Monday evening with a gunnery lecture in the Angel Hotel, Leamington Spa; from Tuesday to Friday the same evening lecture was given at the Shakespeare Room, Warwick Castle; and at 2.30p.m. on the Saturday riding drill was carried out in the castle grounds.[18] By Spring 1909 training, probably aided by the lighter evenings and the men's burgeoning experience, became more diverse:

---

[17] *Warwick Advertiser* 17 October 1908 p.7.

[18] *Warwick Advertiser* 12 December 1908 p.5. The newspaper regularly published the Battery training schedules.

Saturday 17 April – Recruits riding drill 4.30p.m.

Monday 19 April – Gun drill 7p.m.

Tuesday 20 April – Gun drill 7p.m.

Wednesday 21 April – Gun drill and harness fitting 7p.m.

Thursday 22 April – Recruits riding drill 5.30p.m.

Friday 23 April – Recruits riding drill 5.30p.m.

Saturday 24 April – Drill order under Adjutant in Warwick Park 3.30p.m.

Lord Brooke had taken great pains to see that 'his' battery was as well trained as possible and he spent a lot of time administering the Battery with the permanent staff. A distinctive cap badge was introduced for officers: the Royal Artillery cap badge inscribed motto of 'Quo Fas et Gloria Ducunt' was replaced with 'Warwickshire Royal Horse Artillery'.[19] On 25 March 1909 the Battery underwent a full inspection by Lord Brooke, accompanied by Lord Lucas (head of the Territorial Force) and General Sir H MacKinnon (Director General of the Territorial Force). The latter commented that if '... the enthusiasm and energy on the part of the non-commissioned officers and men were anything to go by [the Battery's] success is assured.'[20] Lord Lucas echoed these remarks and praised the Battery for attaining the standard and efficiency it had in such a short time. The day closed with a dinner hosted by Lord Brooke for all ranks, now numbering 180, at Shire Hall, Warwick. The dinner was followed by a smoking concert and a presentation by Sergeant Major Waters, on behalf of all ranks, of a silver model of a 15 Pounder gun to Lord Brooke to celebrate his forthcoming marriage to Elfreda Marjorie Eden in London on 19 April 1909.[21] The wedding – one of the society weddings of the year – resulted in the Battery's first ceremonial duty. On the couple's return to Warwickshire from London they were met at Leamington Spa railway station by a mounted gun detachment that escorted them to Warwick Castle.

It was not until the end of 1909 that the Battery was equipped with its full complement of guns: 'It has been notified that the Warwickshire RHA at Warwick,

[19] This was not, however, exclusive to Warwickshire RHA, Yorkshire's West Riding RHA had a similar arrangement as did some Territorial Force Royal Field Artillery batteries.

[20] *Herald* 2 April 1909 p.3.

[21] Brooke's bride was the sister of Anthony Eden who was to become the local Conservative MP and later Prime Minister and whose brother would later serve as Battery Commander of Warwickshire RHA.

and other units of the Territorial RHA, are to be armed with the new 15 pounder quick firing Erhardt gun.'[22] The much delayed issue of these guns would have pleased all concerned. The 15 Pounder was hardly a 'new' gun, having been purchased from Germany at the time of the Boer War whilst a new generation of field guns was being developed by Britain. But the gun had been updated to British Army requirements to provide a 'quick firer', a gun that did not require re-laying (re-aiming) after each round was fired. In theory this could produce a rate of fire of 20–30 rounds per minute, although 12–15 rounds per minute would be more realistic. And it was the first equipment of the Royal Artillery to incorporate a full recoil system. The 15 Pounder was a light equipment (a little over one ton), highly manoeuvrable and, together with its ammunition limber, was drawn by six horses. The gun fired a shrapnel shell[23] weighing 14 pounds to a maximum range of 6,400 yards. Ten men comprised a full gun detachment: six manned the gun in action, the other four were reliefs or casualty replacements, one of whom was the second-in-command of the detachment (called the coverer). The coverer, as well as being a relief for the Detachment Commander, was responsible for the horse teams in the wagon lines and the preparation of ammunition in the two wagons belonging to the gun in the Ammunition Column. Additionally there were three sets of three drivers (one for the gun team and two for the ammunition wagon teams). Therefore, a complete sub-section totalled 19 men and 18 horses.

By early-1910 the number of volunteers in Warwickshire RHA totalled 183. A breakdown was published of the local towns of the men: Warwick 83, Coventry 43, Stratford-upon-Avon 26, Henley in Arden 26 and Coleshill 5.[24] It is unsurprising that the largest group was from Warwick (this number would have included those from Leamington Spa) as they were closest to the headquarters. It is noteworthy that other towns in Warwickshire (for example, Nuneaton, Rugby, Southam, Alcester and Shipston-on-Stour) did not make up the numbers and that, geographically, Warwickshire RHA was composed of volunteers from a central north/south swath of the county (see Appendix C). This may have been for transport reasons or it may

---

[22] *Warwick Advertiser* 25 December 1909 p.5.

[23] The shell (projectile) encased lead balls, or bullets, which were ejected from the shell close to the target by means of a mechanical fuse which would ignite an explosive in the base of the shell. The bullets spread forward onto the target (together with the brass fuse and steel shell). Accurately aimed and with the correct fuse setting the results at the target end could be devastating.

[24] *Herald* 2 April 1910 p.3.

be that the other towns' volunteers had committed themselves to Territorial Force units closer to home. Four sub-sections (a full gun detachment and its wagons) were made up and based at three locations: 'A' and 'B' sub-sections were from Warwick and Leamington Spa; 'C' sub-section from Coventry and Coleshill; and 'D' sub-section (which provided most of the men for the Ammunition Column as well as a gun detachment) from Stratford-upon-Avon and Henley in Arden. Although the Battery was centred on the headquarters at Warwick Castle and that training took place there, the sub-sections organised themselves well in their respective towns as will be seen. This would have instilled a sub-section pride and doubtlessly brought about inter-sub-section rivalry and competition within the Battery.

By early-1910, the Battery had become a competent unit and its training had developed. The basic lectures, gunnery and horsemanship training had now expanded to include semaphore signalling, carbine training, harness fitting, driving and fuse setting. The Battery's in-house training would be put to the test in May 1910 when it undertook its first annual training camp on Salisbury Plain. The Battery would be exercising with its supported cavalry units:

> The 1st South Midland Brigade has its headquarters at Warwick, and is commanded by Colonel the Hon. OV Lumley. The Camp will be attended by the Warwickshire Yeomanry, the Worcestershire and Gloucestershire Yeomanry Regiments, while on this occasion the Warwickshire RHA Battery, under Lord Brooke, will also train with the Brigade.[25]

The camp was to take place during Whitsuntide which for the yeomanry regiments had been normal practice for many years, rather than exercising during the summer months. (This arrangement would have far reaching consequences come August 1914.) The cavalrymen would have taken the prospect of annual camp in their stride, but for the new men of Warwickshire RHA it must have been a daunting, as well as an exciting, prospect.

By Spring 1910 the Battery was up to strength less two officers for the Ammunition Column and two officers for the Battery. One officer post that was

---

25 *Warwick Advertiser* 29 January 1910 p.5.

not empty was that of Chaplain. The Reverend WG Melville, vicar of Stratford-upon-Avon, was the nominated Chaplain to the Brigade, but he took a particularly keen interest in all activities of Warwickshire RHA and attended each of its annual camps and did much welfare work for it when the Battery went to war. Melville had no problem in obtaining leave of absence to attend the annual camp, but for the men there was no legislation in place for employers to release them to complete annual training: permission had to be sought. It can be supposed, though, that due to the government's emphasis on military expansion and efficiency and for patriotic reasons few employers would have baulked at such absence. But application had to be made nonetheless: 'The porter [of the Stratford-upon-Avon workhouse] applied for leave of absence to attend the annual training of the RHA.'[26]

Preparations complete for the Battery's first annual camp, it was formally inspected by General Sir John French at Warwick Castle on 21 April 1910. The inspection was a complete success. French had visited the Battery previously and he and Lord Brooke were on very friendly terms. Presumably by this time the Battery had received its contracted horses,[27] but some would have been supplied by the soldiers and officers themselves, but these would hardly have been harnessed and used for haulage. It is testimony to all those involved that the military horses would have been unknown to their riders and little familiarisation time would have been had, but they handled them well.

The Battery entrained at Warwick railway station and travelled to Salisbury Plain in Wiltshire. The camp was a great success:

... [The] culmination of annual camp was a battle on Wednesday 19 May. Based around Windmill Hill, an artilleryman reports "... up at 5.30a.m. and in the saddle at 8.30. We had a great field day, and have just returned home – 7.30. This has been the best work the Battery has ever done. It is very hot, but the men returned home looking very fit. The country round here is magnificent. We have done twenty to thirty miles today."[28]

---

[26] *Herald* 13 May 1910 p.6, reporting upon the meeting of the Board of Guardians at the Workhouse on 6 May 1910.

[27] The horses employed by the Royal Horse (and Field) Artillery were Light Draught 1 (for gun towing) and Light Draught 2 (for wagons); their equivalents are Welsh Cob and Irish Draught.

[28] *Warwick Advertiser* 21 May 1910 p.5.

Things were not so good for Lord Brooke '... who returned from manoeuvres late on Wednesday night limping very badly, and was walking lame on Thursday morning [when] he took his Battery out for gun drill.'[29] Lameness aside, the Battery had had a very successful camp and returned to Warwickshire in high spirits.

Gemmell, the Adjutant, had been promoted to major in April 1911. Although Lord Brooke was the *de facto* Battery Commander, Major Gemmell, to all intents and purposes, actually ran the Battery. His place as Adjutant was taken by Captain WA Murray, another regular officer who was posted to the Battery from 115 Battery RFA.

Premises had been identified in Leamington Spa for a permanent headquarters for the Battery after the War Office had purchased a large end of terrace property at 9, Clarendon Place.[30] In addition to having all the requirements for a headquarters the accommodation would also allow for a social club for members. It was anticipated that the new headquarters would be opened by Sir John French in April 1911 but such thoughts were premature. It was not until 16 December 1911 that the General opened the headquarters officially.[31] As well as the officers and men, many dignitaries attended and listened to a long address by French after he had inspected the men. The new headquarters, as well as providing everything needed for a headquarters building also comprised gun sheds, a drill hall, a harness room, and a yard. Inside the building was an officers' club and a soldiers' club (which included a snooker table, used for many inter-unit competitions) and the two top floors accommodated Battery Sergeant Major Waters and Sergeant Instructor Thompson – very spacious and comfortable for these two permanent staff, but something of a come down after Warwick Castle!

It is obvious that an *esprit de corps* had been formed within the Battery as, in addition to their weekly training commitments, the men had entered into a social life based upon their sub-sections. Coventry's 'C' sub-section raised a very good rugby team and 'A' and 'B' sub-sections of Warwick and Leamington Spa played football to a very high standard – a sport at which the Battery would

---

29 *Warwick Advertiser* 21 May 1910 p.5.

30 The building was until recently occupied by Wright Hassall, Solicitors.

31 The premises had been converted by a local builder, RP Gathercole, at an expense of £1,556 to which was added a further £70 by the Territorial Force Association for furnishings.

excel.[32] 'D' sub-section formed 'The Stratford on Avon and Henley Royal Horse Artillery [sic] Rifle Club' of which Reverend Melville was Chairman. They competed against civilian and military teams in the area and were very successful, except (perhaps unsurprisingly) when shooting against the infantrymen of the Royal Warwickshire Regiment. It seems likely that the men had to buy at least some of the ammunition for these competitions as Reverend Melville and the Stratford mayor, Alderman Deer, promised to purchase 100 rounds each from their own pockets.[33] The best shot in 'D' sub-section was Sergeant AB Smith, the Battery's comedian and natural entertainer, who would later become one of the mainstays of the Battery.

The Battery's second annual training camp was held at West Down North, near Tilshead on Salisbury Plain. This time they were not to exercise with the cavalry (which had its annual training of 1911 in Conwy, Wales) but with other Territorial and regular Royal Artillery batteries. This was a good chance to see how the professionals did things, to receive expert guidance from the gunnery staff of the School of Artillery at Larkhill nearby, and to socialise with kindred spirits. The training would take the form of gun drills, technical live firing and 'fire and movement' exercises; the latter seemingly quite realistic:

> The drills in which the Royal Warwick Horse Artillery [sic] have been engaged during the past two or three days have been of a very practical nature and have consisted chiefly of advances from position to position under conditions as near as possible approaching actual warfare.[34]

After three years the part-time gunners were now doing what they had trained for: firing live artillery. What these volunteers thought of their first experience of artillery firing is not known, but almost certainly they would have been impressed with the powerful effects of concentrated fire upon a target area;

---

[32] Football was the Battery's strength: 'There are several local footballers in the Warwickshire RHA... Gunner R Wilday... he is an old Leamington Junior League player... Jack Key, the old Town Football Club forward; John Duran and Ted Checkley and "China" Hill.' (*Warwick Advertiser* 15 January 1916 p.5.) Wilday was wounded on 29 December 1915.

[33] *Herald* 3 February 1911 p.8, reporting on the first Annual Meeting of the club held at the drill hall of the White Swan Hotel in Stratford.

[34] *Warwick Advertiser* 10 June 1911 p.7.

these, of course, were the days when most horse and field gunners were actually in sight of their targets. And it would have been a salutary lesson for the men to realise that much of the gunners' role in warfare was to silence enemy artillery batteries, so called 'counter battery fire': they too could be on the 'receiving end' of such devastating fire....

In addition to their military training the men played sports against the other units attending the camp; whether it was cricket or football Warwickshire RHA were always victorious. In fact, it was at football that the Battery really excelled. Some fine footballers were within the ranks and, as will be seen, even when the Battery was on the Western Front time would always be made for a game. But it seems the highlight of the camp was a fancy dress competition which included representations of the Mayor of Stratford-upon-Avon and an elephant![35]

In high spirits the Battery returned to their Warwick Castle base for the final time and prepared for the move to Clarendon Place. Once in place in Leamington Spa it is probable that the Battery's new training ground would have been Midland Oak Park, about half a mile from the headquarters between Leamington Spa town centre and Lillington. Spring of 1912 was spent preparing for the next annual camp which would be held near Aldershot. This camp was not to include artillery live firing practice, the government having decided that such expense could only be allowed in alternate years. This probably led to some frustration for all concerned. A frustration that was shared by the Earl of Denbigh who, in the following year took up the Territorial Force artillery's case:

> ... he [took] the government to task about only allowing TA artillery units to one firing camp in alternate years. '... I do say empathetically that it is quite impossible to adequately train the huge mass of Territorial artillery we have at the present moment unless the politicians, who apparently insist on having so much of that arm, will also provide the money for sufficient gun ranges and ammunition... the annual gun practice is the most important feature of

---

35 *Warwick Advertiser* 10 June 1911 p.7.

the year's work. Let a battery know that it is not going to practice [live firing] that year, and I will undertake to say that the attendance to drill and the general interest in the proceedings will fall off woefully.'[36]

Denbigh's misgivings will have been shared by many, but his prediction of a lack of interest did not come about, at least not within the ranks of Warwickshire RHA. There seems to have been a change in the Battery's regimes now that it was in a new headquarters and under the (ostensible) command of Major Gemmell.

Prior to the Battery's annual camp, training was stepped up and emphasis was placed on attendance because of the forthcoming camp and new procedures in gun laying drills. New developments in drills and procedures show that the Battery was keeping itself abreast of practices within the regular army and was therefore up to date.

Fully prepared for the camp the Battery entrained for Aldershot on 18 May 1912, where the men would spend a fortnight under canvas. They were accompanied by a Special Correspondent who reported:

Hard slogging and heavy showers and brilliant sunshine has been the lot of Warwickshire RHA who are spending what they hope will be a profitable and pleasant period of training in the Aldershot Command: profitable in the sense that a fortnight devoted to drill will make them as efficient as any unit in the Territorial Force can be... long days of drill amongst the pine-clad hills in the bracing air of Aldershot is really not hard work at all, but a delightful change from everyday surroundings... the healthy open-air life they are living has done them a world of good physically. The Battery has its full complement of 15 pounder quick-firing guns, with its own wagons and horses... reveille at 5a.m.... and from then until 6p.m. the men have hardly a slack moment... the men have applied themselves assiduously to riding and driving drill, dismounting and unlimbering, and going into action... the afternoons have been devoted mainly to gun-laying and signalling. They handle their guns and

---

[36] *Warwick Advertiser* 12 April 1913 p.5, quoting a letter from Denbigh to *The Observer* [n.d.]. The Earl of Denbigh commanded the Honourable Artillery Company, a Territorial unit, which included two batteries.

horses in a manner that does them infinite credit, and there is no disguising the fact that they are very smart indeed. And no wonder! For the men are as keen as mustard.[37]

The high standard of Warwickshire RHA was widely recognised: 'This is the smartest artillery corps in the Territorial Army, and both officers and men pride themselves on their efficiency...'[38] and upon the men ending their training '... all ranks will return to the Midlands with the knowledge they have won golden opinions from everyone who has seen their work. Not a man has been sick, and not a horse injured in any way.'[39] The Battery had obviously gelled into a very effective unit, one which was comparable with regular units. Comparisons had been made with the Honourable Artillery Company[40] and at one time it was suggested a competition be held between the two units. Whether this was a challenge set up between the two aristocratic commanders – Brooke and Denbigh – of the two organisations is unknown, but no such competition was ever held.

To end the training, a smoking concert was held at the camp with the catering being overseen by Sergeant Calman. Although he had been severely wounded during the Boer War when serving with King Edward's Horse, Calman was '... as good a man on a horse as he [was] in the mess tent.'[41]

On 20 July 1912 the Battery held a Sports Day at Warwick Castle Park, organised by Sergeant Major Waters and the NCOs. This was quite an affair as it was more than an in-house gathering. Music was provided by the band of the 4th Battalion, The Royal Warwickshire Regiment to entertain the many visitors – dignitaries and public alike – who had come to see the sport, and the pipers and dancers from the Cameron Highlanders introduced a non-local treat. The events included tent pegging (where a rider attempts to remove a tent peg from the ground with a lance), wrestling on horseback, 100 and 200 yards sprint, rouse-

---

[37] *Warwick Advertiser* 25 May 1912 p.8.

[38] *Warwick Advertiser* 25 May 1912 p.8, quoting from the *Evening Standard* [n.d.].

[39] *Warwick Advertiser* 1 June 1912 p.5.

[40] With the formation of the Territorial Force the Honourable Artillery Company (HAC) formed 'A' and 'B' Batteries HAC to support the London Yeomanry Cavalry Brigades.

[41] *Warwick Advertiser* 25 May 1912 p.8. Calman's predecessor in charge of catering had, unfortunately, been lost with the Titanic the month previously.

and-turn-out, tug-of-war, the Victoria Cross race, mounted Section jumping, recruits off-saddling race and a marathon race (in light marching order). The day was enjoyed by all and was reported in the local press.[42]

The remainder of the year was spent at normal weekly training and consolidation of the Battery in its new headquarters. Everything was running smoothly until in December 1912, Captain Murray, the Adjutant, sustained a serious accidental shooting injury to the face. A London specialist was unable to save his eye (which one is unknown) but he was able to continue in his role.

The Battery received notice that its annual camp of 1913 would again be held on Salisbury Plain and that live firing would be included. The 1st South Midland Mounted Brigade would attend: the Warwickshire, Worcestershire and Gloucestershire Yeomanry regiments, Warwickshire RHA, the Brigade Supply and Transport Columns and a Field Ambulance. The Battery would train exclusively with the units it would deploy with if they should go to war. The training would, as usual, take place over Whitsuntide from 10th to 24th May.

Lord Brooke was to relinquish his post of Battery Commander after the 1913 camp. He had been asked by the Canadian government to command the 2nd Canadian Cavalry Brigade in Canada and quickly accepted the request. He left the Battery after a successful, if rather uncomfortable, training period. The exercising, based on Hamilton Camp, Salisbury Plain, was under the control of the Directing Officer, Colonel Lawrence, who '... put the battery to a severe test, and was well pleased with the manner in which they came into action.'[43] Lord Brooke left the Battery at the end of the training and he, and probably the rest of the Battery, would have been glad to see the last of Salisbury Plain: 'The Larkhill camp is in a most exposed position, and the continuous high and cold winds have taken most of the pleasure out of life under canvas.'[44]

The annual training for 1914 was held in May and June at Aldershot and was therefore a non-firing exercise. No reports have been found to show what form the training took, but it must be assumed that no untoward incidents took place

[42] *Warwick Advertiser* 27 July 1912 p.3, which included the names of attendees and the results of the (somewhat enigmatic) events.

[43] *Warwick Advertiser* 24 May 1913 p.3. It would seem that Lawrence found some shortcomings with the Battery however: although the Battery's gun drill was impeccable, after its return to Leamington Spa the weekly training schedules included a great deal more foot and rifle drill.

[44] *Warwick Advertiser* 24 May 1913 p.3.

and that – once again – the Battery had succeeded in everything it was set. Little did the men of the Battery know that this was to be their last annual training camp and that before the end of the year they would be at war, firing their guns in anger.

Chapter Two

MOBILISATION AND WAR OPERATIONS

When Great Britain declared war on Germany on 4 August 1914 Warwickshire RHA was mobilised immediately. How word was got to all members of the Battery so quickly can be only be guessed at, but on Wednesday 5 August every man of the Battery assembled at the Leamington headquarters to await orders. '... [Warwickshire RHA] mobilised on Wednesday, and there were exciting scenes near the Headquarters... The men turned up to a man and all looked well...'[1] (The roll of the Battery's personnel on mobilisation is at Appendix A.) Among their number were attached personnel from the Medical Corps, the Veterinary Corps and the Service Corps, personnel who had not been identified as attached previously and probably weren't. The organisational machine of war mobilisation set up by Haldane had begun working and it is likely that these attached personnel had been earmarked earlier to join Warwickshire RHA in just such an event. The men bedded down in the headquarters and drill hall and the following day a church service was held in the yard of 9 Clarendon Place where Reverend Melville addressed the men. The following nine days were frenetic, with everyone engaged in the preparation for deployment and all men were medically examined. Permission was given to those who needed to return to their homes to arrange personal, family and business matters prior to movement.

It was now that Warwickshire RHA became 1/1 Warwickshire RHA (TF).[2] Soon after, a second Warwickshire RHA battery (2/1) began recruiting in Warwickshire with Major Lord Ivrea as Battery Commander. 2/1 Battery would

---

[1] *Warwick Advertiser* 8 August 1914 p.8.

[2] Why the Battery assumed '1/1' and not '1' or '1st' is something of a mystery, all county RHA batteries also carried the same title.

deploy to France in mid-June 1917 and see active service until the end of the war. A third line unit (3/1 Battery) was later raised in Leamington Spa from which replacements for 1/1 and 2/1 Batteries were drawn.

On 14 August the Battery mustered on Midland Oak Park, near Lillington and rode down to Leamington Spa railway station bound for Bury St Edmunds, Suffolk.[3] Once in East Anglia the Battery was based at Grove Farm near Thurlston, nearby was the remainder of the 1st South Midland Mounted Brigade. The men were billeted in local houses until a marquee tented area could be set up and messing was done at the Fox and Hounds public house. It is obvious that the Battery was not fully equipped at this time as the day after its arrival the Ammunition Column was issued its full complement of horses.[4] Ammunition for the guns and small arms was issued and all was made ready for war operations. The remainder of August was spent exercising and undertaking emergency drills to check preparedness: 'At 1.15a.m.... the alarm was at once sounded and the battery and column had to harness up and turn out in the dark...'[5] (The Battery was ready to move in 63 minutes; the Worcestershire Yeomanry took 3½ hours!)

On 31 August the Brigade, under the command of Brigadier-General EA Wiggin, moved by rail to Newbury in Berkshire where it was based upon the racecourse which had been recently surrounded by barbed wire as it was intended to use the space as a prisoner-of-war camp during hostilities. The Brigade, which had become part of 2nd Mounted Division under Major General WE Peyton, remained in Newbury for two months, and was made up of approximately 2,000 men (and not much fewer horses). Where possible men were billeted in local houses but most were in tented accommodation in and around the racecourse. It was at this time that the men of the Battery were canvassed with regard to deployment on the continent; hitherto they had been a home defence force and their terms of reference required them to volunteer for overseas service. This was 'crunch' time for the Battery; the men could stay at home and perform

---

3   In mid-2007 the author spoke with a 101 year old lady who was born in Leamington Spa and was eight at the time. She could remember vividly the Battery making its way through the town as people lined the streets. In particular she remembered the noise of the horses, guns and limbers: 'a rattling, rumbling noise, very loud, and dusty, too... all was horse traffic, of course.'

4   In peacetime Ammunition Columns were nearly all under strength.

5   Shakespeare Birthplace Trust Records Office (SBTRO) DR 325/1184 (and 1185), the diary of Corporal Harry Fox of the Ammunition Column, entry for 22 August 1914.'

home defence duties or they could follow the British Expeditionary Force (BEF) to France and oppose the enemy there. The vote was 100% for France: and so 'In a field at Thatcham, near Newbury the battery volunteered to a man for Active Service...'[6] The 100% vote is noteworthy and must say a lot about the morale and dedication of the Battery members. Other Territorial Force units achieved as little as a 30% volunteer rate.[7]

September was spent in the preparation for the move to France. All were inoculated, probably against cholera. And leave was taken as required. All ran smoothly except for a furious stampede of the Brigade's horses on 12 September; several horses had to be destroyed after about 2,000 bolted and ran amok through the streets of Newbury.[8] October arrived and the men waited for embarkation and, in preparation for their time on the Western Front, they were treated to some foul weather. The Battery area at the racecourse was practically flooded in mid-October and all had to be moved to a firmer, drier place. The weather notwithstanding the Brigade was inspected by the King and General Sir Ian Hamilton at Churn.

It was in October that the Battery received bad news: it was to be left behind:

> Considerable disappointment was caused... by the announcement that the battery... was to be left behind, its place being taken by a battery of the Hon. Artillery Company, under Lord Denbigh. However... word was brought that the battery was... to be attached to a regular cavalry brigade for active service at the front. The guns of the HAC were handed over to the Warwick Battery and an entirely new outfit of saddlery and harness was fitted in two days.[9]

Although the Battery had been fully equipped and ready for deployment to the continent it is strange that an apparent swap of equipment was made with 'A' Battery HAC. Since its foundation the Battery had always been praised for its

---

[6]   From 'A Note on the Battery' within the Order of Ceremony for the dedication of the Warwickshire RHA memorial, Midland Oak Park, Leamington Spa, 7 October 1967. (Leamington Spa Public Library Local Studies Department).

[7]   When this was the case, those wishing to remain at home would have been taken on strength of their second line units.

[8]   This was a very serious stampede; it is believed that a horse of the Warwickshire Yeomanry had been startled by a passing motor car. As well as injury to the horses, much damage was caused to property in Newbury. (See *Warwick Advertiser* 19 September 1914)

[9]   *Herald* 6 November 1914.

turn-out and high standards, which undoubtedly was the case; but there is a suggestion here that its guns and at least some of its other equipment was not up to the required standard. The atmosphere must have been very tense between the two batteries during this period:

> Early in October ['A'] Battery [HAC] received its first great shock. Owing to the keenness of RSM HA Terry, the equipment was complete... to the last gaiter button. Orders were promptly received, not to proceed to France, but to hand over all equipment to Warwickshire RHA, an order which was carried out with the greatest reluctance.[10]

The two batteries were similarly equipped with the 15 Pounder Erhardt gun and all ancillary equipment, so why should a complete exchange of equipment (and it would seem it was a *complete* exchange) take place? These were orders from the War Office, not from Brigade or Divisional level. It is quite possible (and very probable) that Lord Brooke, by now in France and on the personal staff of his old friend Sir John French, the commander of the BEF, had used his influence to ensure that *his* battery would be at the front as soon as possible – and better equipped than previously.

The Battery was taken on strength of Headquarters, British Expeditionary Force and left behind old friends in the Yeomanry regiments and overnight on 30/31 October 1914 sailed from Southampton to France with the 3rd Dragoon Guards on board the *Victorian*, arriving at Le Havre in the early evening of 31st. Disembarkation and unloading took place '... on 1 November, thus [making Warwickshire RHA] the first Territorial artillery unit to enter active service in the First World War.'[11] Had Lord Brooke achieved his aim? For the majority of the Battery this was the first time that any would have been to a foreign country and seen and heard the different sights and sounds that such travel gives. The countryside and crops in the fields impressed most of the men, it '...seemed impossible to realise that [the] country was at war.'[12] The men soon adjusted to

---

[10] G Goold Walker (ed.) *The Honourable Artillery Company in the Great War 1914–1919* London, 1930 p.109.

[11] NDG James *Before the Echoes Die Away: The Story of a Warwickshire Territorial Gunner Regiment 1892–1969*, 1980 p.30.

[12] SBTRO DR 325/1184, entry for 3 November 1914.

the new experience as, *en route* to their first holding area, the local vintage was being enjoyed.[13]

The Battery moved by rail to St Omer, where it was met by Lord Brooke,[14] and then marched about three miles to Esquerdes where the men billeted in the area about a mill. Although some way from the front artillery fire could be heard and the presence of freshly made graves assuredly concentrated minds. Settled in and awaiting orders the Battery encountered every soldier's adversary: the weather. They were no longer in a tented encampment on Salisbury Plain but sleeping where and how they could; rain followed rain and soon the ground was a quagmire. A move to better ground proved as bad and eventually the horses were picketed on the road. If the men found the conditions hard the horses suffered more so, with many becoming sick and others dying. The horse sick-lines were manned constantly with both veterinary staff and Battery men caring for the mounts. The weather must have had some effect upon the horses, but there is a possibility that their general condition was not good enough for the rigours of such a life. The bad weather and lack of food for humans and animals made life uncomfortable – but the debilitating lack of sleep soon affected the men. Snatched hours, here and there, was all they could expect and usually their slumbers were taken under a single blanket in wet and severe cold.

During this period Lord Brooke accompanied Sir John French on an inspection of the Battery. As personal secretary and friend to the Commander-in-Chief, Brooke would have been proud to show off the battery to which he was so sentimentally attached. Although by now the Battery would have been less presentable than at inspections in Warwickshire!

The men of the Ammunition Column spent a great deal of time searching far and wide for fodder for the horses and were in competition with other units in the area. At times the mayors of local towns requisitioned potatoes and fodder for the allied effort, but as the huge logistical machine that was to provide for the field army was not yet fully in place, it was for the time being a case of 'independent' catering. The demand for fodder was great and throughout the war

---

13 SBTRO DR 325/1184, entry for 3 November 1914: '... old friend G Brown announced... his 26th birthday and his health was obviously drunk in a bottle of vin blanc.'

14 At the war's commencement Brooke had returned from Canada and re-joined French's staff. Brooke's wife travelled to France shortly afterwards and worked as a nurse on hospital trains.

the supply could be sporadic – the Battery had to beg fodder from other units on many occasions.

On 14 November, Field Marshal Lord Roberts died, aged 82, at St Omer.[15] He had come out of retirement as commander of Indian troops in France and was in transit to visit those already at the front. His body was repatriated to London on 17 November, prior to which was a simple funeral ceremony in St Omer. 1/1 Warwickshire RHA was selected to provide the gun carriage, horses and men to convey Roberts' coffin from 52, Rue Carnot to St Omer town hall for the obsequies. There was a truly international flavour at the ceremony with not only the Battery gun carriage and flower-festooned limber, but French and Indian cavalry units acting as honour guards and British infantry lining the route of the procession. The local population are reported as having been indifferent to the proceedings, but this was a large military ceremonial occasion. But why had 1/1 Warwickshire RHA been selected for the duty when there would have been regular Royal Artillery units, well versed in ceremonial duties, nearby? The suspicion is that Lord Brooke 'volunteered' the Battery to French, whose duty it was to provide a fine military farewell to the late hero.[16]

The remainder of November and early-December was spent in routines of gun drills, inspections, church parades and reviews, and attending the horses which were in a very poor state with as many as 12% in the sick-lines. The weather had been appalling with much rain and freezing conditions hardly breaking during the day but at the beginning of December the men received greatcoats and more winter clothing which may have alleviated some of the discomfort, but for most boots, saturated and frozen solid, were the order of the day.

On 4 December the Battery joined the 2nd Cavalry Division where it would provide artillery support, together with 'D' Battery RHA, to 4th Hussars, 5th Lancers, 6th Lancers, 3rd Dragoon Guards.

---

[15]   Field Marshal Lord Frederick Sleigh Roberts, VC (1832–1914) was the epitome of the Victorian national military hero whose portrait hung in many houses alongside the monarch. He spent much of his service in India and Africa and had won his Victoria Cross as a young artillery officer in India.

[16]   The day was miserable; all on parade were soaked to the skin and bitterly cold. Any 'spit and polish' would have been superficial – some men actually washing from the rainwater in the gutters just prior to the parade. An unknown Battery member wrote to the *Warwick Advertiser* (5 December 1914 p.5) giving the names of the detachment that performed the duty: Lieutenant Woodhouse, Sergeant Hayes, Bombardiers Glover, Pickard and Southey, Gunners Neil, Cope and Checkley. The drivers were Bombardiers Dodd, Smith and Clarke. (Checkley would be Mentioned in Dispatches in 1918 for his 'general good work.')

The Battery began its move towards the front, encountering sporadic aerial bombardment along the way, but it was not until mid-December when it went into action near Billieux. If any of the men had believed the claim that the war would be over by Christmas, they would surely have been having serious misgivings about the prediction by now. Less than a fortnight before the festivities would begin at home the Battery's crews were unhooking their guns, preparing gun platforms, unloading ammunition wagons and un-boxing ammunition, getting horses and wagons away and making everything ready for their first engagement. At 10.10a.m. on 13 December 1914 Sergeant Hayes and his crew fired 1/1 Warwickshire RHA's first operational round. Six years of training had been brought to a climax with this initiation of fire. How many men in the Battery ever thought, when they signed on, that they would experience such a thing? The Battery's Rubicon had been crossed: they were no longer 'amateur' players but were now deep into the most murderous war to date. Any memories of firing over Salisbury Plain could now be cast from their minds as the targets there were not human beings; from now on the men had to have an attitude of total dispassion regarding those on the receiving end of their fire.

Chaos reigned for the Battery on 15 December. The men of the Ammunition Column became lost during re-supply and found themselves amongst British artillery batteries which were receiving counter-battery fire from German artillery: '... took a wrong turning and we were soon in the thick of firing. Within 20 yards of 4.7 [inch] guns when they were firing. Jack Johnsons and shells bursting all round us and we were warned to get out as we were in great danger. Eventually we found our way, passing about 20 batteries in action.'[17] The Battery gun line, near Fleurbeuse, fared worse. The guns were positioned with other artillery batteries and came under intense counter-battery fire from two enemy heavy batteries. So sustained was the fire that the men were forced to retire from the guns to safety. Eventually the German batteries were silenced by counter-counter-battery fire from a British 4.5 inch battery. First hand accounts of this action, probably made due to the novelty of being shelled for the first time, give interesting (and darkly amusing) insights into this action.

---

[17]   SBTRO DR 325/1184, entry for 16 December 1914. 'Jack Johnsons' were German shells that produced large quantities of black smoke upon detonation, named after Jack Johnson, the negro heavyweight world boxing champion 1908–1915.

Captain, the Earl of Clonmel, now commanding the Ammunition Column, had withdrawn to the shelter of some buildings to the rear of the gun position which were immediately shelled; he opined that the quick switch of fire had been directed by fifth columnists rather enemy aerial spotters. He recorded that the Medical Officer with him had had his overcoat shredded by shell splinters from an impact on the roof of their sanctuary and that a soldier who had been cooking a steak by the side of the building had been flung into a cesspool![18] In a letter home Bombardier Arthur Dodd described the action: '... we took the teams and gunners' horses out of range in double quick time... I'm as happy as ever I was. This war has got into my blood, and I'll never complain, come what may... if ever men needed prayers it is the British infantry. Theirs *is* a life and no mistake...'[19] (Although the weather took its toll on the Battery, with either frozen ground or knee-deep mud wherever it went, Dodd's recognition of the appalling straits of the infantryman is humbling.) Amazingly, the Battery suffered no casualties during this intense shellfire.

The weather continued to spare no one but still the horses suffered more than the humans with some having to be sent back to veterinary depots for treatment or destruction. Few comforts could be afforded the men as they spent Christmas in reserve, although a welcome issue of new underwear was made. As well as presents from home the men were sent warm clothing; Reverend Melville had organised the ladies of Stratford, and even schoolgirls, to make knitted woollens for their local horse artillery battery:

> The Girls' School has sent... to the Warwickshire Royal Horse Artillery, a very nice parcel of beautifully knitted woollen gloves... The Vicar proposes to get together a Christmas parcel for the Battery, and will be glad to include and forward any special gifts from friends to Stratford Gunners and Drivers.[20]

---

[18] *Warwick Advertiser* 20 February 1915 p.5, quoting a letter sent by Clonmel to some ladies. It is a shame the identity of the soldier chef is unknown, having shown such *sang froid*.

[19] *Warwick Advertiser* 26 December 1914 p.3. Arthur Dodd was invalided back home in May 1916 suffering from pneumonia.

[20] *The Stratford-on-Avon Parish Magazine* vol xxxv no 12 (December 1914) Regulation sizes for the woollens had to be strictly adhered to: mittens were to be 9½ inches from cuff to fingertip and scarves 58 inches long and 9 inches wide. Donors' attentions were drawn to the need for dull colours – it is tacit that some of the ladies had been enthusiastically artistic in earlier efforts! The Christmas parcel, although despatched in time, went astray in the post and arrived with the Battery in mid-January 1915.

Mid-January 1915 saw the Battery back in action in old infantry trench systems at La Couture which were prepared into gun pits during lulls in firing. The Battery was in action all month and fired a total of 409 rounds.[21] Throughout this time re-supply of stores, food, water and ammunition had to be made by the Ammunition Column (usually at night) whose role is easy to overlook. Ammunition scales were 176 rounds per gun in the battery and 220 rounds per gun with the Ammunition Column. Extra ammunition had to be drawn from divisional dumps as expenditure reduced the battery-held stocks and it was the Column's job to go and fetch it, wherever the dumps may be. Theirs was an arduous and dangerous business.

Rather strangely Belgian refugees seem to have been living side by side with the Battery taking the dangers of the front line in their stride, but probably happy to do so as the gunners would have shared their rations with them.[22] Evening times would be spent with music and dancing with these displaced people. Once the Battery's work had been done, it was withdrawn for rest. Rain, cold and snow made the rest period uncomfortable with men and horses vying for shelter wherever it could be found. Routines were kept up with exercising and inspections of horses and equipment. Football matches were arranged with other units in the rear areas. Church services were assiduously attended and as many men as possible were sent home on leave.

On 14 April 1915 the Battery transferred to VII Brigade RHA, 9th Cavalry Brigade, 1st Cavalry Division but it was not until late-May 1915 that it would be brought into the line again. Although having moved forward to the Ypres/Hazebrouke area for large scale offensives, the Battery was held back. A lot of the Battery personnel, including Battery Commander Major Gemmell, fell victim to a localised measles outbreak at this time, but even so, time was found for football matches against other units and even horse shows were held.

---

[21] This was not a lot of ammunition, but when it is considered that some batteries were rationed to how many rounds that could be fired daily due to shortages of ammunition (some sources suggest as few as 2 rounds per gun per day), it was above average expenditure.

[22] In a letter to his family dated 22 January 1915 which was printed in the *Herald* (5 February 1915 p.5), Corporal Fox described the conditions there at the time, conditions the Belgians seemed happy to endure:
'We have fired hundreds of rounds into the German lines, and no doubt have done considerable damage... There are batteries with us, both heavy and field guns, and you can imagine the din that goes when all are firing... As I write I can distinctly hear the ping of the rifle bullets from an attack that is going in on our immediate front.'

During the evening of 24 May 1915 the Battery occupied a gun position half a mile from Ypres, next to 'I' Battery RHA and with the infamous Hill 60 to its right. The move had been a slow affair; with much congestion on the roads as there were many troops moving to the front, among them '... Algerian cavalry (very fine) [and]... infantry, rifle in one hand, shovel in the other.'[23] From the outset the Battery position and the wagon lines (a mile to the rear of the guns and located with the Royal Scots and Royal Highlanders in their rest areas) came under heavy German artillery fire. The men wore respirators in case the Germans had mixed gas shell with the high explosive and shrapnel shell. Again, and to everyone's astonishment, no casualties were sustained within the Battery.[24] It is as if the men of 1/1 Warwickshire RHA were living charmed lives – after six months in the most murderous of operational areas the Battery was intact.

After two days the Battery (less 'D' sub-section which was left in action for a time) withdrew to the rear for rest and training. The men were not allowed to be idle. Regular work parties were sent to the front to assist in digging field works and entrenchments, leaving their colleagues to clean and maintain equipment and exercise the horses, which were healthier for the summer weather – even though the rain gave little respite.

9th Cavalry Brigade was inspected by French, the Commander in Chief, on 15 June when he thanked everyone for the hard work they had been doing. He would not have been accompanied by Lord Brooke at this inspection as Brooke had been promoted and was now commanding 4th Canadian Infantry Brigade.[25]

Although in the rear, the Battery was on permanent stand-by to return to the front at three hours notice, but this did not prevent the men being able to march to nearby Wormhouldt for baths and clean uniforms. What a pleasure that must have been for them! Exercises, gun drills and mounted drills helped pass the time as did regular church services and regimental band concerts. And some of the

---

23 SBTRO DR 325/1184, entry for 24 May 1915. It is interesting to note the esteem with which foreign and imperial troops were held by Fox and his colleagues; whether British, French, Algerians, Indians or Canadians, all worked very well together in the struggle against the common enemy.

24 'We got the guns into action, and coming back [to the wagon lines] the Germans started shelling us... I thought our time had come... We are the only battery that has taken that position without a casualty.' From a letter to the *Stratford-upon-Avon Herald* from Sergeant Alfred 'Doc' Smith (writing as Dr A Smith) dated 24 May 1915 and printed 18 June 1915 p.5.

25 Lord Brooke was severely wounded in late-1915 and would never take to the field again. After his recovery he continued with Canadian troops by commanding a Canadian Training Brigade on Salisbury Plain.

men were examined by a board for possible commissioning.[26] Not all of the candidates were successful. In fact, Sergeant Alfred 'Doc' Smith, the Battery Quartermaster, refused a commission (he had actually re-enlisted with the Battery whilst in France to see the war to its conclusion in the ranks). Although by now rested, clean and well fed, the men were continuously aware they were still in a war zone: artillery fire could be heard and occasionally German interdictory fire passed over their heads towards targets deep in the allied rear echelon.

In mid-July 1915 the Battery undertook intensive training in river crossings near Morbecque with the Battery achieving a record 1 hour and 17 minutes for moving the entire battery and Ammunition Column across a canal (beating the average time of 1 hour 30 minutes). Swimming and tug-of-war was enjoyed in, and over, the canal; the men never missed an opportunity to enjoy themselves.

On 2 August the Battery, with the rest of the Brigade, went to the seaside for a 'holiday'. *En route* manoeuvres were carried out before arriving in Mardyk about 4 miles from Dunkirk. For three days the men enjoyed bathing in the surf, the cavalry officers raced their mounts along the sands and a local *estaminet* was drunk dry – literally.[27] The weather, as wet as ever, didn't seem to dampen the men's spirits.

Returning to rest areas the Brigade was tasked with digging trenches at the front (a job that would last six days) about 3 miles from Poperinghe. The work was done in shifts 24 hour a day and throughout, but particularly at night, enemy harassing artillery fire preyed upon the diggers. The horrors of harassing shellfire were matched by the horror of what was sometimes dug through. At one point the trench system being dug was through a graveyard and skeletons were being disinterred regularly, with some having to be cut in half to keep the line of the trench. At times the men were witness to full scale attacks against the German lines and had to shelter from spotter aircraft as well as enemy fire. Exposed and hardly armed, the men must have felt impotent whilst digging the sodden ground. At one point the wagon lines of 9th Brigade was shelled resulting in 4 dead, 49 wounded with casualties among the horses. But once again, the Battery remained unscathed.

---

[26] About 229,000 new commissions were granted in World War One, almost 108,000 had passed through the ranks. (See Richard Holmes 'View from the Ground' in *The Guardian Literary Review* 11 November 2006 p.21.) By war's end some of 1/1 Warwickshire RHA had been commissioned, some taking up posts within the regular army.

[27] SBTRO DR 325/1184, entry for 2 August 1915. 'Estaminet near sea front soon drunk out of beer, and men started to drink wine and spirits and drunk place dry. Very wet night, slept in open, wet through.'

A posed photograph of three members of 'A' sub-section with their gun during a lull in firing on Salisbury Plain, c.1912. (Photo: Ray Westlake Unit Archives.)

The Battery marching along Newbold Terrace, towards the Parade, Leamington Spa, c.1912. This is probably a church parade. The two officers on the right of the picture are possibly Captain Gemmell (left) and Lord Brooke (right) and the tall, be-medalled figure at the centre of the picture is almost certainly BSM Freddie Waters. (Photo: Leamington Spa Courier, 29 November 1985; courtesy of the Editor.)

Headquarters, 9, Clarendon Place, Leamington Spa. (Photo: P. Spinks.)

An open page of the book cataloguing the names of the First World War dead of 1/1 and 2/1 Batteries. (Photo: P. Spinks.)

The memorial plaque at Midland Oak Park, Leamington Spa. (Photo: P. Spinks.)

Warwick Castle, the Battery's first headquarters. (Photo: P. Spinks.)

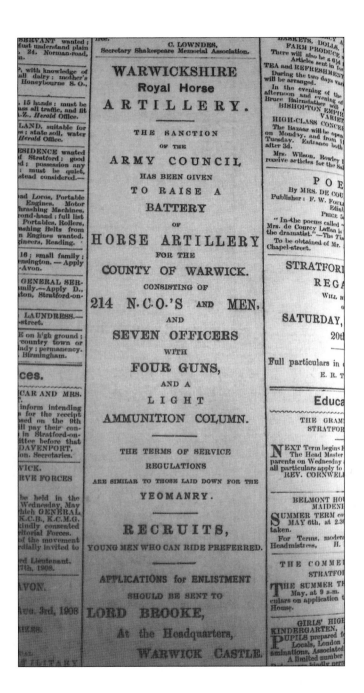

A newspaper recruiting advertisement for men to join the Battery.
(Stratford-upon-Avon Herald, 1 May 1908; courtesy of the Editor.)

The funeral cortege of Field Marshal Lord Roberts at St Omer on 17 November 1914.
(Photo: Courtesy Garen Ewing, Second Anglo-Afghan War Collection,
www.angloafghanwar.info)

But two days later Lieutenant Woodhouse, a popular officer, became the Battery's first fatality: late at night he '... was killed by an explosive shell. It appears that Lieutenant Woodhouse and a Belgian officer were standing near a trench mortar when a shell dropped between them and "wiped them both out"'.[28]

Digging duties over, the Battery began to re-train on another type of gun – the 13 Pounder Quick Firing field gun – prior to delivery of new guns to replace the tired 15 Pounders. This British made gun had been used by regular Royal Horse Artillery batteries since 1904. A gun was borrowed from 'H' Battery RHA for the training. On 23 August 1/1 Warwickshire RHA's new guns arrived from England. But instead of the 13 Pounders that had been expected the Battery received four 18 Pounders, guns normally employed by Royal Field Artillery batteries, those batteries which supported infantry. This gun fired an 18 pound shell to a maximum range of 6,250 yards;[29] in addition to the improved performance the gun could fire a high explosive shell (one which detonates on impact with the ground) as well as the standard shrapnel round. A few days were allowed for familiarisation (the 18 Pounder and 13 Pounder were very similar in many respects and re-training would have not been needed) and gun drill prior to active deployment.

At the beginning of September, along with other RHA batteries ('D', 'E', 'G', 'H', and 'I' Batteries), the Battery began a fitful move to the front. Work parties were sent forward to prepare gun pits at Les Brebis before the guns could be positioned. The area was in mining country; the water was black with coal dust and although the men were happy to wash in it drinking water for men and horses had to be brought from afar by the Ammunition Column in water carts. The Battery went into action on 6 September and began firing almost immediately with ammunition being re-supplied at night. Consolidation of gun pits was done in breaks during the firing with reinforcement being made with stone, steel girders, wooden beams, bricks and earth to a depth of six feet. All guns were connected to the Command Post (from which orders were sent by voice down rain water hoses!) by trenches, some of which ran through the cellars of houses. Lessons had been learned

---

[28]   *Herald* 3 September 1915 p.5.

[29]   This range could be increased to 8,000 yards if the single trail of the gun was dug into the earth, giving a greater elevation to the gun.

with regard to counter-battery fire: dig in and keep covered! For ten days the Battery remained in constant action in what was a strong, and comparatively comfortable, position before being withdrawn.

Only a short time was allowed the men to clean their equipment and themselves, including having their clothing, equipment and small arms disinfected and being given an ointment to rub onto their bodies as a lice deterrent, and re-organise before taking up exercises with the cavalry to practice what would be done when the German line was broken during the next major engagement of the war: the ill-fated and very costly Battle of Loos. Once again the move to the front was fitful; the roads were heavily congested with other units on the march. And once again, after six days of travelling the Battery found itself, along with the supported cavalry of 9th Brigade, in reserve.

On 25 September 1915, the Battle of Loos commenced. This was to be the biggest land battle for the British Army up to that time with about 800,000 men committed. And the first time that the British would use gas as a conventional weapon of war.

The men of the Battery would certainly have heard the offensive from their billets in railway rolling stock at sidings near Arles, officers in the carriages, other ranks in the cattle trucks, which was probably the best accommodation they had had since arriving in France ten months previously. (Unfortunately each morning the train would depart for its day's work and not return until the evening, meaning all personal equipment had to be unloaded for the day.) Nearby was a large hospital used for military casualties and the cavalry and Battery sent working parties to assist in the wards or in burial details: this was disconcerting, but necessary and worthwhile work.

The constant search for shelter, by all those at the front, seems to have been more important than the quest for food – any shelter was welcomed and the reserve areas, in which 1/1 Warwickshire RHA found itself all too often, where thousands of troops, their equipment and horses harboured must have taken on the form of shanty towns with everyone wanting to keep warm and dry.[30] This nomadic

---

[30] SBTRO DR 325/1184 entries from 23 September – 4 October 1915. In his diary Fox recounts sleeping out for six nights in rain, then in railway cattle trucks, another night in the open, then in an ammunition wagon, a railway booking office and finally, having found 'Very bad billets; had a hunt round and found an empty room in a cottage. Best sleeping place for some weeks.' His experience would have been typical.

experience would have been almost bearable if it were not for the fact that no one knew, or could even speculate, how long hostilities would continue. Only a few days leave could be hoped for to relieve the endless discomfort whilst under constant threat of injury or death from interdictory or harassing artillery fire.

The 9th Brigade moved constantly around the rear areas, moving from billet to billet, and always in reserve. Newcomers arrived at the Battery from England. Nothing has been discovered to suggest that any but Warwickshire men, or at least men who lived in Warwickshire, served with the Battery in its earlier operational years and it is therefore likely that these new arrivals were from 2/1 Warwickshire RHA in Leamington. The new soldiers were given training and exercising and gun drills were carried out where possible during the desultory movement around the countryside. By the end of October the Battery was withdrawn to its winter billets and was quartered at Sequires, about eight miles from Boulogne. But before long, constant movement from reserve billet to reserve billet began again. Eventually the Battery came into action in December to support various actions. The wagon lines were at Noeuf les Mines and nightly re-supply was carried out from there. Casualties were sustained from counter-battery fire, including the Medical Officer, wounded in the head and others who were buried in the cloying mud: 'One of our men in trench up to his waist, had to cut greatcoat in half to get him out. Bodies buried in mud and hands and legs sticking out.'[31] Withdrawn for rest, the Battery spent Christmas near Haillicourt. Christmas Day was very wet, but this did not dampen the spirits, especially in the wagon lines where champagne was the order of the day. But festivities were marred when 'C' sub-section, sleeping in a cellar, received a terrific shock (but no fatalities or severe injuries) when a German shell found its way into their hideout on 27 December.

The men returned to action and spent a 'settled', but dangerous, period in action at Le Philosophe between Bethune and Lens until mid-February 1916. On 23 February the Battery again moved to the rear and billeted at Halighen near Boulogne. A fortnight later another move brought the men to Samer. Although men had been lost to enemy action, the Battery was required to send 30 men to

---

31 SBTRO DR 325/1184 entry for 7–9 December 1915.

augment a Royal Field Artillery battery that had sustained greater casualties. The late-winter and early-spring was spent in training and consolidation for the Battery and changes were made in the officer ranks. On 26 March 1916 Major Gemmell left the Battery (on promotion to Lieutenant Colonel) and his position as Battery Commander was taken by Major Murray, previously the Battery's adjutant. Three months later, the local press reported: 'Major WA Murray commanding Warwickshire RHA has been awarded the DSO [Distinguished Service Order]. He writes most glowing accounts of his Battery, which has been very heavily engaged, and has suffered terribly in both men and officers... Colonel Gemmell DSO, who took them [the Battery] out, is in command of a Brigade of RFA...'[32] The phrase 'suffered terribly in both men and officers' should be read in context. By the time of this report the Battery had sustained just two fatalities (Gunner H C Collingbourne from Coventry and Lieutenant Woodhouse), the number of men lost wounded or sick is unknown, but is likely to have been high. The reason for the seemingly low casualty rate is that the Battery supported cavalry, an arm that had not been used as widely as had been anticipated at the war's start. (What must also be taken into account is the number of men who finished their four year engagement and left the Battery to return home.) Compared with other RHA and RFA batteries 1/1 Warwickshire RHA had, until this time, fared quite well. But the time would come when the Battery *would* 'suffer terribly'.

Leave was taken by all who were entitled to it or to those who had been deprived of it due to operational needs – an all too common occurrence. In addition to their duties of internal re-supply of fodder and stores, the Ammunition Column was detailed to convey parcels for French prisoners-of-war (presumably) for the Red Cross. And, as usual, the Battery's football team was performing well, it having progressed to the final of the 1st Division Cup on Easter Monday and beaten the Ambulance Park 1–0. The members of the team each received a silver matchbox and 20 francs from General Mullins.

Still in reserve, the Battery remained near Samer until mid-June 1916. Also at this time a further two guns were received making the Battery a six gun unit. It

32 *Herald* 22 June 1916 p.3.

is not known how many new men arrived, if any at all, to man the extra equipment and horses, and it is quite possible that the Battery was stretched. But it must have been near to its full establishment because on the evening of 24 June 1916 the Battery began a long and slow move to the front together with the rest of 1st (to which the Battery belonged) and 3rd Cavalry Divisions. By 0600 the following day Douriez had been reached, a distance of 30 miles had been covered in just nine hours – a good rate when darkness, poor roads and other busy traffic is considered. By day the Battery harboured and for four days this movement by night and resting by day, in almost constant rain, continued lest German spotter aircraft should identify the huge troop movements that were afoot. Finally the two divisions based themselves at Querrieu, the headquarters of 4th Army, and although the headquarters staff was probably well catered for, the field units were hard pressed: '... [the] village entirely taken over by troops... no bread, bully or biscuits.'[33] Preparatory artillery fire would have been heard by the men but no one in the Battery would be aware that they were on the verge of the British Army's worst ever day: the first day of the Somme.

At 0045 on 1 July 1916 the Battery moved forward to the front and halted at La Vieville, about four miles from Albert. Again the Battery found itself in reserve, stood to amongst the flood of front-bound troops and rearward-bound casualties. Harry Fox recorded the passage of wounded and intimates the enormous logistical preparations made for this huge attack: 'On [the] way back a great number of wounded passed us, and a railway, specially built for the attack, brought down a great train of trucks (about 100 trucks in all) filled with wounded.'[34] The Battery was withdrawn to the rear, and again placed in reserve at Querrieu where it remained for nearly a week when 1st and 3rd Cavalry Divisions were ordered further back due to congestion in the area. Again and again the divisions were drawn further to the rear until by 10 August, over six weeks since their initial moves to the Somme battle, they arrived near the coast with Dieppe and Treport close by.

And there they remained until 6 September when 1st Division was ordered forward with the Battery eventually coming into action nine days later when it

33 SBTRO DR 325/1185 entry for 29 June 1916.
34 SBTRO DR 325/1184, entry for 1 July 1916.

suffered casualties. For nearly two months the Battery remained in action and was finally withdrawn to reserve with the 1st Cavalry Division.

On 29 November 1916 1/1 Warwickshire RHA transferred from 1st Cavalry Division to 29th Divisional Artillery. It took the place of 'Y' Battery RHA in XV Brigade RHA alongside 'B' Battery RHA, 'L' Battery RHA and 460th Howitzer Battery RFA. Although the Divisional Artillery War Record[35] gives the details of the exchange, it does not give a reason why it should have happened. However, an officer with 1/1 Warwickshire RHA at the time (GRG Mure) recalled that the exchange was at the Battery's own request.[36] This seems a strange request, but one that was granted by higher command. What brought about the request is not known, of course. The only thing that 1/1 Warwickshire RHA had in common with 29th Divisional Artillery is that both the Battery and the Division were formed and trained in Warwickshire. But when the 29th Divisional Artillery was formed in Leamington Spa in January 1915, 1/1 Warwickshire RHA had been in France for two months and would have had no direct dealings with it. And there is the possibility that the Battery was feeling left out of things and the chance to swap to supporting an infantry division would give it more experience and the chance of more action. Whatever the reasons may have been this exchange was to be a watershed for the Battery – following its association with 29th Division it would sustain over ninety *per cent* of its war fatalities.

The Battery was soon in action at Leuze Wood, near Combles (having taken over a position from the French) where the weather conditions and the mud were appalling. The deep mud had, however, its advantages at times even though the conditions overall were bad: 'Ground by guns in a terrible state, shell holes every few yards. Aeroplanes bomb us one night and [we] are shelled the next. *Ground so soft do little damage...* mud dreadful and men get stuck and have to be helped out.'[37]

Christmas 1916 was spent in action but on 28 December the Battery with XV Brigade was sent to rest at Morlamourt. The Brigade's 18 Pounder guns were left *in situ* and were manned by men of XVII Brigade RFA (13, 26 and 92

35 RM Johnson *29th Divisional Artillery War Record and Honours Book 1915–1918* Woolwich, 1921 p.191.
36 NDG James *Before the Echoes Die Away* p.31. Much of the book's chapter on 1/1 Warwickshire RHA was compiled from Mure's unpublished notes about the Battery.
37 SBTRO DR 352/1185, entry for 9–15 December 1916 [my italics].

Batteries) until 8 January 1917 when the guns were reunited with their owners. On 27 January Sergeant Ackerman received a Mention in Dispatches for '... great gallantry and coolness in charge of battery signals... near Le Transloy, when he repaired lines in the open under heavy shell fire.'[38] The Battery would remain in action until mid-March, but in February 1917, during a particularly hard freeze, the Battery encountered technical difficulties: the guns were firing short of the targets and dropping rounds amongst their own infantry due to the very low temperature of the propellant inside the ammunition cartridge cases. 'Higher authority always regarded the 18-pounder gun as a more precise weapon than it was...' GRG Mure,[39] a lieutenant with the Battery recalled, and after a delegation from the War Office visited to look into the matter, additional corrections were made to the range tables for the 18 Pounder: '... you had now not only to reckon for the wind and air temperature, but put a thermometer up the hole in the bottom of the [cartridge] case and take the temperature of the propellant.'[40] (It is hoped that the corrections applied by the 'boffins' improved relations between the gunners and their supported infantry.)

XV Brigade assembled at Morlamourt in mid-March and began a six day move to Gouves in order to prepare gun positions near Arras. Once in position the Battery began registering targets for the forthcoming large scale attack that would see the commencement of the Battle of Arras. On 9 April, during the attack, which began in a snowstorm, the Battery moved forward with the infantry from Cojeul to the Scarpe where its actions were noted by Lieutenant Colonel Sherbrooke, commanding XV Artillery Brigade:

The Warwickshire Battery RHA... was in action at St Sauveur, close to Arras, firing the barrage in support of the attack that day... within 1200 yards of our front line. A heavy, hostile barrage was put down [upon the Battery]... and two complete detachments and two officers [were] killed. The Battery continued firing, supporting on three objectives, from 5.30a.m. to 3.30p.m., advanced that

---

[38] RM Johnson *29th Divisional Artillery Record* p.20.

[39] GRG Mure had remained in Leamington Spa to assist with the formation of 2/1 Battery and joined 1/1 Battery in September 1915. He was to become the most decorated of the Battery members and served on the General Staff from 1939–1945.

[40] NDG James *Before the Echoes Die Away* p.32. Measuring the charge temperature, and making adjustments to the gun's range accordingly, has since been standard practice.

night in the dark, supported a further attack next morning, and advanced again that afternoon to Fuechy Chapel, where that night it again had a whole detachment knocked out and had to change position the next day, but remained in action.[41]

The Battery had shown much vigour during this period of intense activity and although by now undermanned and quite possibly under equipped (although no mention is made of loss of guns) it was still in a position to continue in action. In this one action the Battery lost more men killed than in its previous 26 months in France; the grievous shock felt by the men must have been tremendous but, quite literally, they 'stuck to their guns' and followed the attack. And it was here that the Battery's first Military Medals were won:

Warwickshire RHA were heavily engaged during Easter week, and, as a consequence, many men were killed and wounded. The Battery did splendid work and... Corporal Norman Kinman... has been awarded the military medal [sic] for conspicuous gallantry, being the first member of the Battery to gain the distinction.[42]

Kinman '... under heavy fire and with disregard for his own safety [had] continued to serve his gun notwithstanding the next gun [having] received a direct hit killing 10 and wounding 5.'[43] At the same time Sergeant Roxburgh earned his Military Medal when he '... was in charge of a gun in action. Although the gun next to his was knocked out and his own detachment had many casualties, he maintained his gun in action under very heavy shelling, and carried out his programme of fire all day.'[44]

Soon after this action the Battery were brought back to reserve and a well earned rest but on 1 May 1917 it joined 460th Howitzer Battery where it supported an unsuccessful attack by 3rd Division. Four days rest in mid-May was

---

[41] RM Johnson *29th Divisional Artillery* p.196.

[42] *Herald* 25 May 1917 p.3. Kinman was a particularly fine footballer. Perhaps the *Stratford-upon-Avon* Herald was being partisan by claiming that Kinman's MM was the first in the Battery. Kinman was a Stratfordian, Sergeant Roxburgh was not (see below).

[43] RM Johnson *29th Divisional Artillery Record* p.37.

[44] RM Johnson *29th Divisional Artillery Record* p.46.

followed by another return to action for nearly a month and then the whole of XV Brigade undertook an eight day move to Houtkerque.

Major Murray left the Battery on promotion in mid–June 1917 and handed over command of the Battery to Captain (later Major) The Hon. RE Eden. Eden was to command the Battery for the remainder of the war.[45]

(In mid–June 1917, 2/1 Warwickshire RHA moved to France as part of CXXVI Brigade RFA and would stay with that brigade until the end of the war. 2/1 Battery took part in the Third Battle of Ypres in 1917 and the Forcing of the Drocourt-Quéant Line in 1918. The men were not to meet up with 1/1 Battery until after the war ended.)

From 14–17 July the Battery was in action near Elverdinghe. During this time a captured Prussian officer claimed that the Brigade's barrage had been '... "absolutely rotten." He could not explain, though, that seeing how poor the Brigade's shooting had been he had surrendered.'[46] A fortnight later the Battery was in action at White Hope Corner, near Elverdinghe when the Acting Battery Sergeant Major, C Bull, was in charge of ammunition re-supply during the night of 27/28 July when:

> ... the road east of Elverdinghe [along which the ammunition team moved] was under fire from 5.9 inch and gas shell. BSM Bull kept his party together with courage and coolness and succeeded in delivering his ammunition and getting his party back safely; he also managed to extricate and bring back a wagon which had been hit and overturned.

For his leadership and control on that night Bull was awarded the Military Medal and, later, the French Croix de Guerre. Bull went on to be commissioned later in the war.

The Battery was soon preparing for an attack and advance onto Broenbeek. From 8–15 August the Battery suffered heavy counter-battery fire and on 10 August particularly accurate enemy fire caused havoc in the position on the bank of the Ypres Comines Canal near Boesinghe: two guns were put out of

---

45 Brother-in-law to Lord Brooke and brother of Anthony Eden, later Prime Minister, who himself was serving at the front.

46 RM Johnson *29th Divisional Artillery Record* p.196.

action, camouflage nets were set ablaze, another gun was set on fire and ammunition began exploding. All detachments were removed to the flank of the position and:

> ... 2nd Lieuts. Philip and Malby, with Sergeant Kinman and Gunner Dixon, worked for twenty minutes under continuous shell fire, with ammunition continuing to explode, until all fires were extinguished and the guns recamouflaged. By this prompt action a large quantity of ammunition was saved and the guns preserved from further damage.[47]

For these courageous actions the two officers were awarded the Military Cross, Gunner Dixon received the Military Medal and Sergeant Kinman was awarded a bar to his Military Medal earned earlier in the year.

At this point the guns of the Brigade were firing as little as ten rounds *per* gun *per* day due to ammunition shortages. Ammunition was available at the main ammunition dumps but it could not be brought to the batteries in quantity, there being no roads and almost impassable mud. And when the Ammunition Column was able to replenish the guns it was a dangerous business.

An artillery battery is as good as the men serving in it. Accurate and timely fire can only be delivered through teamwork, which depends upon discipline, experience, willingness and good morale – qualities which 1/1 Warwickshire RHA held aplenty. One of the men who kept up the Battery's spirits throughout its campaigning years was the Battery Quartermaster Sergeant Alfred Bennett Smith. He had been the Battery's entertainer and comedian since its birth and had paid particular attention to the welfare of the men at all times. As has been mentioned Smith had refused a commission and had actually re-enlisted with the Battery during the war to see the fight to its end. On 12 August 1917 Sergeant Smith:

> ... volunteered to go up to the Battery with ammunition, and on the way back the party was shelled. Your son [Smith] heard a shell land in the rear and went

---

[47]   RM Johnson *29th Divisional Artillery Record* p.14.

back to see if the men and animals were all right, when another shell came and killed him. We are all very, very grieved by his death.[48]

The former Battery Commander, now Lieutenant Colonel WA Murray and commanding XVII Brigade in 29th Divisional Artillery, wrote to Smith's parents likewise:

Our friendship has extended over a good many years... no one better than I knows how much he did for the welfare of every man [in the Battery]... he was a tremendous help in showing the younger men how to bear the discomforts and bad times with a light heart and smiling face... he treated danger with the same jocular cynicism that he treated discomfort and up to the last I don't think he paid any more attention to a shell than to a snowball ... there will be a gap which will never be filled.

Although the Battery had sustained many fatalities and casualties, the loss of Sergeant Smith, aged 39 years, shook all ranks: Murray's words spoke for them all.

To make matters worse, there were accusations of shells falling short and that failures to fire on SOS targets had occurred.[49] Although the Brigade was in action an inquiry was undertaken and it was found that during ten minutes of constant firing only one gun had fired short and that all SOS calls had been fired upon. The Brigade had been absolved and the operation had been successful.

Rest was taken during the first fortnight of September 1917. From 14–17 September the Battery was preparing to support an infantry operation for a projected two weeks. Into action at Hey Wood, the Battery was issued with 875 rounds *per* gun. During the operation counter-battery fire was heavy and included gas, particularly at night. There was also heavy aerial bombardment and

---

[48] From a letter to Smith's parents from Rev. WJ Hunkin, an Army chaplain, published in the *Herald* 31 August 1917 p.3. Murray's letter was published in the same report. See also Michael Caldwell *For King and Country: The Fallen of Stratford-upon-Avon 1914–1918, 1939–1945* Unpublished work, 2000 pp.97–98. (Copy in SBTRO)

[49] A defensive fire SOS (DF SOS) target was the infantry's life-saver to assist in preventing their positions being overwhelmed by a surprise attack such as a trench raid. The SOS target location would be agreed between the infantry commander and his artillery observer and would likely to have been an enemy forming-up point. Guns, when not engaged on other targets, would be laid and loaded onto the SOS target and fired upon when called to do so.

this caused many fatalities among the horses. Although the men had been hard pressed, once in the rear the spirit of the men seemed undaunted:

> We learn that after a recent hot action the Warwickshire RHA played a football match behind the line, the sides being picked from the right and left sections. Sergeant Kinman was the pivot of the left section, which won by two goals to nil.[50]

The Battery had a quieter month in October, being able to move forward to positions near Steenbeck without enemy artillery fire to contend with; in fact, so disinclined were the Germans to engage targets that the move was made in broad daylight – something that the Battery was quite unused to. When supporting attacks at Langemarck on the night of 22/23 October, Gunner Poole earned the Military Medal when he acted as runner between the observation post and the gun line due to the telephone lines having been cut – a distance in excess of one and a half miles. He not only carried important messages to and fro under incessant shell fire throughout the night, but managed to repair sections of the cable whilst doing so. He had displayed 'conspicuous courage and energy' according to the citation for his award. It is not known if Poole was a member of the Battery football team, but he is likely to have made a good winger!

At the end of the month all the guns and howitzers of the Brigade were sent to ordnance base workshops for a complete overhaul. This was probably well overdue; Warwickshire RHA had not had its 18 Pounders serviced fully since acquiring them nearly eighteen months previously, and although the Battery fitters and wheelwrights would have kept maintenance up to schedule, they had no resources for dismantling the guns. (If the Battery personnel were hoping for a leisurely time now they had no guns, they were to be upset. They were set to digging duties at the front.) After the necessary maintenance the Battery's guns were calibrated at Fricourt artillery range near Albert in the first week of November.[51]

---

[50]   *Herald* 28 September 1917 p.3.

[51]   Calibration is the measurement of the muzzle velocity of the gun, i.e. the speed at which a projectile leaves the barrel; this was done to compensate for wear inside the barrel that is caused when a round is fired through it. It is not known how many rounds each gun of the Battery had fired before this calibration, but it may be safely assumed that the number ran into the thousands.

Following calibration, XV Brigade moved forward to a bivouac near Hennois Wood. The Brigade's task was to support an attack by tanks which would be brought to the front at night by railway. Tentage was in short supply; there were few duckboards; it was wet most of the time and cold all of the time; no lights or fires were allowed – altogether a very uncomfortable time for the gunners. But whilst awaiting its time to attack, the Battery, stood to near a 4.5 inch ammunition dump at a quarry in Gouzeaucourt, came under heavy enemy shell fire which set fire to the dump. Second Lieutenant Mulholland, Corporal Keen and Gunner Perks, still under fire, managed to extinguish the blaze and saved the dump from exploding. Mulholland received the Military Cross and Keen and Perks each the Military Medal.

This was the eve of the Battle of Cambrai – when large numbers of tanks would be used for the first time – but when the attack commenced on the morning of 20 November 1917 1/1 Warwickshire RHA, when moving forward into position, found itself trapped in a sunken road at La Vacquerie that had been blocked by four tanks which had become stuck there. The Battery struggled to extricate itself from the 'traffic jam' and eventually came into action in the Vacquerie Valley.

A huge German counter-attack took place on 30 November and there was very heavy counter-battery fire into the Battery's position which was still in the Vacquerie Valley in an exposed location on a forward slope; XV Brigade's attempts to neutralise the enemy artillery had been ineffective. Prior to the main assault, as a result of the counter-battery fire of high explosive and gas shell, several men were buried beneath the cratered ground. Lieutenant GHS Dixon, whose own respirator had been buried, superintended the digging party to free the men and carried one to safety. Dixon received the Military Cross for his efforts.[52]

In addition to enemy artillery fire, the Battery was subjected to severe aerial bombardment. All lines of communication to the Battery's forward observation posts had been cut and soon allied infantry were retiring through the Battery gun position – closely followed by German infantry. This enemy vanguard was engaged over open sights by the Warwickshire gunners who managed to repulse

52   RM Johnson *29th Divisional Artillery Record* p.7.

the assault – some enemy had actually got as close as forty yards to the gun line! The Battery's ammunition expenditure for the day was about 1,500 rounds. And whereas some of the batteries of XV Brigade had removed breech blocks and sights from their guns (to make them unusable to the enemy in case of their being captured) and retired, 1/1 Warwickshire RHA had stood its ground and had, amazingly, sustained only 2 killed and some wounded.

By the following day the entire Brigade had regrouped at Nurlu and underwent a complete (and much needed) refit. The winter had set in hard and it was by slow moves and a final four day march in deep snow that the Brigade arrived in Aubin St Vaast in time for Christmas which was spent in billets. Whether the men received Christmas presents is not known, but the horses received frost cogs for their shoes to aid traction. Another hard move in early-January 1918 to the Thiembronne area was made by the Battery so that preparations could be made for a ceremonial parade of the Division. However, before the parade and inspection could take place the Brigade was deployed to the Ypres salient and into a camp near Poperinghe where '... [the conditions] baffled description. Even though the units were well accustomed to mud, they certainly experienced something very near the limit in this respect.'[53] (Perhaps the 'spit and polish' of ceremonial preparation held a certain allure to the men at this time.)

Shortly afterwards, and probably to the men's relief, the Brigade moved to Abraham's Heights (Gravenstafel Ridge) to support infantry there. There was little enemy activity and operations were low key. Due to the quiet of the front, men from all four batteries in the Brigade were set to ammunition salvage at the front. From mid-January until mid-February the men recovered ammunition that had been lost, discarded or that had simply sunk into the mud and slime. And it was not only ammunition that the men retrieved. They recovered 14 x 18 Pounder guns; 6 x 4.5 inch howitzers; 9,327 x 18 Pounder rounds complete; 3,507 x 4.5 Howitzer shell; 177 x 60 Pounder shell; 227 x 6 inch shell; 38,366 spent 18 Pounder cartridge cases; and 214 boxes of small arms ammunition. This enormous amount of *materiel* was from a very small area of the front and was certainly not

53   RM Johnson *29th Divisional Artillery Record* p.216.

the entire amount that lay above and below the earth (what would the entire front have given up?) and presents well the horrific scene the countryside must have been then.[54]

After its ammunition salvage duties, the Brigade moved to a rest camp near Poperinghe for three weeks. There must have been more than just XV Brigade in this camp as a knock-out football competition was organised between ten batteries. The prizes were to be specially stamped medals from the Commander Royal Artillery. The final match was between 'B' Battery RHA and 1/1 Warwickshire RHA which ran into extra time and which was won by the latter.[55]

From 8 March until 7 April 1918, the Battery occupied a well defended position on a forward slope of Gravenstafel Ridge which gave a good sweep of the area to its front. On 11 March some 600 enemy assaulted the ridge but were repulsed, due largely to the effective and accurate direct fire from the Battery in its safe location. For the next three months the Battery remained in action, providing desultory fire support to minor operations.

Finally, in July 1917, the Battery was withdrawn to a rest area near Wardreques. Here, on 11 July, the men took part in the Divisional Horse Show and although their footballing opponents from 'B' Battery won the best gun team competition, the Warwickshire gunners walked away with the NCOs Jumping Competition Trophy.[56] But all was not fun and games during this rest period. The men were detailed to provide working parties to prepare positions for forthcoming operations. Once the digging had been completed the operations were cancelled and the fieldworks were abandoned. But this operational

---

[54] An advertisement for War Bonds published in the *Stratford-upon-Avon Herald* (1 November 1918 p.2) gives the price of an 18 Pounder gun as £1,250 and two rounds of ammunition at £5. Therefore, the cost of the recovered 18 Pounder guns and ammunition *alone* amounted to £64,135; this equates to a 2006 price (using the retail price index) of £2,145,967.20!

[55] The Battery football team did not, for once, include Sergeant Kinman. He had been gassed and wounded in December 1917 and had been repatriated to his home in Stratford-upon-Avon. Both Kinman and his wife succumbed to the 'flu pandemic of 1918; Mrs Kinman predeceased her husband by two weeks. Kinman died on 5 November 1918. His funeral was conducted by Reverend Melville and the pall bearers were old Battery members. (See M Caldwell *For King and Country* pp.71–73.)

[56] One of the main exponents of horse jumping in the Battery was Battery Sergeant Major (BSM) Freddie Waters who served with the Battery for most of the war and later became BSM to the Battery's successor unit. It was he who, in 1923, when competing in a jumping competition had his front teeth smashed out when his horse through its head back – but he went on to win his round!

cancellation gave the Commander of 29th Division his chance to inspect finally the entire XV Brigade: with full ceremonial the batteries advanced, trotted past and performed what was required: the inspection was '... a great success from every point of view.'[57]

The Battery returned to action with XV Brigade in August 1918 and were soon supporting infantry attacks on Hoegenacker Hill and Outtersteane. Brigadier General Cheape, commanding 86th Infantry Brigade sent the following message on 18 August: 'My infantry wish to express the admiration of the most perfect barrage which you [XV Brigade] put up today during our attack. There were no shorts and it was like walking behind a wall.'[58] This was high praise indeed!

On the last day of August the Battery deployed in a way it had not done so previously. Rather than positioning their six guns in a battery formation, individual guns were dispersed and brought near to targets (sometimes as close as 50 yards) from where they would pound the objective prior to the infantry storming, thereby minimising friendly casualties.

The final allied onslaught against the enemy began; no longer were the artillery and infantry confined to gun pits and trenches, but were now in full pursuit of a breaking German army. But this was an advance not a rout, with fierce enemy opposition at times. On the night of 5/6 September the Battery wagon lines near Le Veau was heavily shelled with gas, '... many shells bursting close enough to splash the horses with liquid...' a party of men consisting of Sergeant Collingridge, Bombardier Thomason and Driver Ashley '... gallantly managed to move from the area all the 39 horses that were there and put nose-bags on them filled with damp grass. This prompt action saved many horses from serious consequences and set a fine example to the other men.'[59] For their part in this resourceful and brave work, all three men were awarded the Military Medal.

The Battery was in constant action from 28 September until 11 November, keeping pace with, and providing supporting fire to, the advancing allied infantry. The period of 7–11 November was spent awaiting re-supply of ammunition and

[57]   RM Johnson *29th Divisional Artillery Record* p.223.

[58]   RM Johnson *29th Divisional Artillery Record* p.224.

[59]   RM Johnson *29th Divisional Artillery Record* p.20.

a river crossing prior to the *coup de grace* of the enemy opposite, but 'the enemy did not wait for the attack'. The Battery's war operations were drawn to a close. At 1100 hours on 11 November 1918, when hostilities ceased, the Battery was at St Genois. No reports have been found to say how the men of 1/1 Warwickshire RHA celebrated the news of the armistice, or if they did. Nor do we know how they reacted to the news. What they did know was that it was an armistice and not a surrender; therefore fighting could recommence, although the likelihood of that happening was remote.

More awards were forthcoming: from mid–September until the end of the war. Sergeant F W Franklin had held the post of Battery Sergeant Major, during that time he had shown '... persistent gallantry and devotion to duty. His fine example in the most trying circumstances was a constant encouragement to the men, and his ability and leadership contributed greatly to the way in which the battery adapted itself to the conditions of moving warfare.'[60] Franklin gained the Meritorious Service Medal. Battery Quartermaster Sergeant Hayes – he whose gun crew had fired the Battery's first round of the war – was awarded the Meritorious Service Medal for '... exemplary conduct, courage and cheerfulness. His hard and conscientious work has materially contributed to the welfare and efficiency of his battery in which he served in France since 1914.'[61] And Sergeant AG Smith received a Mention in Dispatches: he had proved himself to be '... a first-rate No. 1. His bravery, coolness under fire, and cheerfulness contributed greatly to the high moral[e] of the battery during the final operations in Belgium.'[62] What is special about these three awards is that none were made for particular acts of gallantry (like so many others awarded in the Battery) but were for the examples these senior NCOs had shown to their men and the trouble they had taken over the men's welfare. These men, probably more than anything else, show the spirit that was alive in the Battery, and it was because of such men that that spirit grew and was sustained through four years of shared hardship, danger and, too often, the loss of very close friends.

What the officers and men expected after the cessation of hostilities can only be imagined. But it can be assumed they had expectations of demobilisation and

60   RM Johnson *29th Divisional Artillery Record* p.30.
61   RM Johnson *29th Divisional Artillery Record* p.33.
62   RM Johnson *29th Divisional Artillery Record* p.48.

a speedy return home, they having 'done their bit'.[63] This was not to be. 1/1 Warwickshire RHA with the remainder of XV Brigade and the entire 29th Divisional Artillery were to spend the first six days of peace preparing for the march into Germany. 29th Division was to be the vanguard of the column of the occupying force that would enter Cologne.

The journey, commenced on 18 November, took nearly a month due to the inevitable chaos that is the aftermath of war. But on 13 December 1918 1/1 Warwickshire RHA was one of the first units to march across the Hohenzollern Bridge over the Rhine into Cologne. The Divisional Artillery was based in the Bergisch Gladbach and Paffrath and spent the winter in billets as members of the occupying force. Here the Battery was joined by its fellow Warwickshire gunners of 2/1 Battery.

The 29th Divisional Artillery was wound up on 1 April 1919 and '... all units disappeared in the course of the next few weeks.'[64] Repatriation of Battery men was desultory. It was not until 3 June 1919, nearly eight months after the armistice, that the remaining cadre of 2 officers and 41 men arrived back in Leamington Spa at 9.55p.m. where crowds had gathered at the railway station and the town hall to welcome the men home. The Mayor of Leamington Spa, the Corporation and Reverend Melville welcomed the men officially and they then marched to the town hall led by the Royal Artillery Band, being joined by old Battery comrades and, after a speech by the Mayor all were entertained in the town hall.

Among this returning group were nine men who had left Leamington Spa on mobilisation and who had spent the entire war with the Battery. A tenth was absent however: Major Eden, the Battery Commander, had remained behind in Cologne in command of 2/1 Warwickshire RHA.

---

[63] For an insight into demobilisation arrangements (and passions) see Malcolm Brown *1918 Year of Victory* London, 1998 Ch 12 *passim*.

[64] RM Johnson *29th Divisional Artillery Record* p.232. 1/1 Warwickshire RHA, as a military entity, was disbanded. Two years after the war a new Territorial battery was raised and established at 9 Clarendon Place, Leamington Spa: 271 Battery RFA (part of 68th South Midland Field Brigade).

Chapter Three

MEMORIALS

During the First World War 1/1 Warwickshire Royal Horse Artillery lost 60 men killed in action, died of wounds or of natural causes during the period of hostilities (see Appendix B).[1] Their names are endorsed upon their respective home-town and home-village war memorials throughout Warwickshire and beyond.[2] A memorial dedicated to the combined dead of 1/1 and 2/1 Warwickshire RHA was not commissioned until 1927 when the Earl of Warwick, formerly Lord Brooke, initiated the idea of a memorial plaque.[3] He had always taken a very keen interest in both batteries and the welfare of the men (but particularly 1/1) during and after the war and had, on several occasions, hosted reunion dinners for the men. It was in the Russo-Japanese War of 1904/05 that his '... realisation of the tragic side of war increased his natural sympathy for those who suffered and his interest in those who fought and escaped [death and injury]. He never lost touch with old comrades, nor an opportunity to do them service if it was within his power. He was a true comrade.'[4]

The money for the plaque was raised *via* subscription from old members of the two batteries. The bronze tablet cost £150 and is inscribed:

---

[1] These numbers include *all* Battery members, even if they died of natural causes after they had left the Battery, for example, Sergeant Kinman who died of 'flu in early November 1918. Of the original 224 officers and men (from all arms) who mobilised in August 1914, research has identified 24 killed in action, 3 died of wounds (of 43 reported woundings, some men being wounded more than once), and one – Gunner J Coomes – died from wounds whilst a prisoner-of-war.

[2] For example, Lord Poulett of the Ammunition Column transferred to the Royal Warwickshire Regiment in 1918 and died at his home in Crewkerne, Somerset later that year, where he is memorialised.

[3] Brooke had succeeded his father in 1925. He himself died in January 1928 after a long illness aged 45. He was buried in St Mary's Church, Warwick. At the head of the official mourners were old members of Warwickshire RHA, over 100 of them, led by Colonel Gemmell, DSO. The coffin was carried on a gun carriage, drawn by a team from 271 Battery RFA, under the command of Battery Sergeant Major Waters.

[4] *Warwick Advertiser* 4 February 1928 p.8.

TO THE GLORIOUS MEMORY OF THE OFFICERS,
NCOs AND MEN OF THE WARWICKSHIRE
ROYAL HORSE ARTILLERY WHO GAVE THEIR LIVES
FOR KING AND COUNTRY IN THE GREAT WAR
1914–1919

On Sunday 17 July 1927 over 160 ex-members of 1/1 and 2/1 Batteries paraded at Warwick Castle where they were inspected by Brigadier-General Wiggin (who had commanded 1st South Midland Brigade on mobilisation in 1914), accompanied by Reverend Melville and then marched to St Mary's Church in Warwick for the official unveiling by Wiggin. After the ceremony, all returned to Warwick Castle where they were entertained by the Earl and the ex-officers and Sergeant Major Waters joined the Earl for lunch.[5]

The memorial is on the north wall of the nave of St Mary's Church and beneath it is a casket containing a book recording the names of the fallen preceded by a short history of the two batteries.

★ ★ ★ ★ ★

Forty years later a memorial to Warwickshire RHA was unveiled in Midland Oak Park, Lillington Road, Leamington Spa. This was a fitting site as this was where 1/1 Warwickshire RHA had mustered prior to the march to Leamington Spa railway station in August 1914. On 7 October 1967 Lord Avon (Anthony Eden) unveiled a bronze tablet embedded in a granite boulder in the presence of 50 survivors from the two batteries. Lord Avon, who had served on the Western Front himself, and whose brother had been the last Battery Commander said of the men of the batteries during his address: 'The selflessness of their conduct and action, as well as the devotion with which so many gave their lives for their country in a harsh ordeal is in itself the proudest possible memorial.'[6]

---

5   WCRO CR 1886/Box 893/5. Documents relating to the memorial. This collection includes letters from officers replying to the invitation to the unveiling. It seems that two committees, one for officers and one for Other Ranks, sent out the invitations; none of the replies from the Other Ranks have been found.
6   *Warwick Advertiser* 13 October 1967 p.4.

The memorial is inscribed:

WARWICKSHIRE ROYAL HORSE ARTILLERY T.F.

FLANDERS 1914
COLOGNE 1918

TO ALL WHO SERVED
LEST WE FORGET

UNVEILED BY RT. HON. EARL OF AVON K.G., M.C. 1967

At the centre of the memorial is the Royal Artillery cap badge.

The memorial was re-sited a few yards from its original position on 15 March 2003 to make way for a drainage scheme. In a re-dedication ceremony a 'Tree of Heaven' (*Gingko biloba*) was planted behind the memorial.

Appendix A

1/1 WARWICKSHIRE RHA ROLL ON MOBILISATION – 5 AUGUST 1914

BATTERY HEADQUARTERS
Gemmell WLS, *Major (BC)*
Murray WA, *Major (Adjutant)*
The Earl of Clonmel, *Captain*
Woodhouse C, *Lieutenant*
The Earl Poulett, *Lieutenant*
Peto RA, *Second Lieutenant*
Eden, The Hon RE, *Second Lieutenant*

Clayton, *Lt Medical Officer*
Seldon, *Lt Veterinary Officer*

BATTERY PERSONNEL
Waters F, *WO2 (BSM)*
Cowler, *BQMS*
Croton, *Sgt*
Megainey, *Sgt*
McGragor, *Sgt*
Parks, *Sgt*
Scampton C, *Sgt*

BATTERY PERSONNEL (Cont.)
Ackerman, *Cpl*
Horswill TA, *Cpl*
Reeves, *Cpl*
Spencer CH, *Cpl*
Spencer W, *Cpl*
Bull C, *Bdr*
Chattaway, *Bdr*
Clark, *Bdr*
Dodd, *Bdr*
Healuck, *Bdr*
Roxburgh, *Bdr*
Smith, *Bdr*
Trahern, *Bdr*
Ashmore, *A/Bdr*
Collingridge, *A/Bdr*
Deamon, *A/Bdr*
Eaton H, *A/Bdr*
Franklin FW, *A/Bdr*
Hobley, *A/Bdr*

BATTERY PERSONNEL (Cont.)

Parker, *A/Bdr*

Wheatley, *A/Bdr*

Sharp, *Trumpeter*

Partridge, *S/Sgt Farrier*

Shirley, *Cpl Shoeing Smith*

Ford, *Shoeing Smith*

Ford HE, *Shoeing Smith*

Bleasdale J, *Gnr*

Bleasdale F, *Gnr*

Bell, *Gnr*

Boyes, *Gnr*

Barnes H, *Gnr*

Barham, *Gnr*

Caldicott, *Gnr*

Cope, *Gnr*

Checkley E, *Gnr*

Croft, *Gnr*

Croydon, *Gnr*

Cowley, *Gnr*

Collingbourne HC, *Gnr*

Carter ST, *Gnr*

Chain, *Gnr*

Davis FE, *Gnr*

Davis J, *Gnr*

Deamon VE, *Gnr*

Edmunds G, *Gnr*

Eaton C, *Gnr*

Fletcher, *Gnr*

Fitzgerald P, *Gnr*

Farmer, *Gnr*

BATTERY PERSONNEL (Cont.)

Gardner G, *Gnr*

Guise, *Gnr*

Grubb, *Gnr*

Hornsby, *Gnr*

Hall JW, *Gnr*

Irving G, *Gnr*

Jackson P, *Gnr*

Keen GHM, *Gnr*

Key, *Gnr*

Lamb, *Gnr*

Maynard, *Gnr*

Neale, *Gnr*

Nicholls, *Gnr*

Nichols, *Gnr*

Ollerenshaw, *Gnr*

Phillips, *Gnr*

Persons EH, *Gnr*

Perks, *Gnr*

Reynolds, *Gnr*

Robinson RH, *Gnr*

Randall, *Gnr*

Robertson, *Gnr*

Southley, *Gnr*

Winyard, *S/Sgt Saddler*

Clarkson, *Saddler*

Hayes, *Cpl Fitter*

Durran JT, *Wheeler*

Hill J, *Wheeler*

Avery, *Gnr*

Anstey, *Gnr*

BATTERY PERSONNEL (Cont.)

Pickard, *Gnr*

Merriman, *Gnr*

Sharland, *Gnr*

Goss, *Gnr*

Bentley, *Dvr*

Baker, *Dvr*

Bennett, *Dvr*

Crowther, *Dvr*

Cookwell, *Dvr*

Cowley, *Dvr*

Elsworth, *Dvr*

Dee, *Dvr*

Deeley, *Dvr*

Franklin, *Dvr*

Howkins, *Dvr*

Hubbard, *Dvr*

Hammond, *Dvr*

Poole, *Dvr*

Pugh, *Dvr*

Porter, *Dvr*

Russell, *Dvr*

Rollason, *Dvr*

Smith HA, *Dvr*

Shilcock, *Dvr*

Slater, *Dvr*

Spencer HB, *Dvr*

Thamason, *Dvr*

Williams J, *Dvr*

Williams L, *Dvr*

Tuck, *Dvr*

BATTERY PERSONNEL (Cont.)

Thomson, *Dvr*

Tatlow, *Gnr*

Gardner H, *Dvr*

Johnson, *Dvr*

Heath, *Dvr*

Stanley, *Gnr*

Bold, *Gnr*

Wilkinson, *Dvr*

Payne, *Dvr*

Noonhan, *Dvr*

Hotchin, *Dvr*

Keen F, *Dvr*

Coomes, *Dvr*

Rutler, *Dvr*

Launchbury, *Dvr*

Smith AG, *Dvr*

Hancock, *Dvr*

Shelly R, *Gnr*

Wilday F, *Gnr*

Ward, *Gnr*

Westwood, *Gnr*

Glover, *Gnr*

Morris, *Gnr*

Reed EE, *Gnr*

Gerrish, *Dvr*

Horrocks, *Dvr*

Morgan, *Dvr*

AMMUNITION COLUMN

Smith AB, *Sgt*

Harris, *Sgt*

Moore, *Sgt*

Cortigan, *Cpl*

Smith T, *Cpl*

Grub, *Cpl*

Fox H, *Cpl*

Woolern, *Bdr*

Thorneloe, *Bdr*

Read FD, *Bdr*

Dent J, *A/Bdr*

Davis T, *A/Bdr*

Harrison, *A/Bdr*

Checkley, *Trumpeter*

Morby, *Shoeing Smith*

Davis A, *Shoeing Smith*

Houlton, *Sgt Saddler*

Moore, *S/Sgt Saddler*

Jenkins, *Fitter*

Brown, *Gnr*

Bailey AW, *Gnr*

Grose, *Gnr*

Pugh HC, *Gnr*

Durran, *Gnr*

Facer HA, *Gnr*

Woodfield, *Gnr*

Keen F, *Gnr*

Megainey, *Gnr*

Mellwain, *Gnr*

Clarke, *Gnr*

AMMUNITION COLUMN (Cont.)

Bailey WV, *Gnr*

Barwick, *Gnr*

Biddle, *Gnr*

Clarke FE, *Gnr*

Lewis GA, *Gnr*

Kinman N, *Gnr*

Baker, *Gnr*

Bastock, *Dvr*

Gloster, *Dvr*

Middleton, *Dvr*

Hewitt, *Dvr*

Rose, *Dvr*

Wightman, *Dvr*

North, *Dvr*

Cole, *Dvr*

Trench, *Dvr*

Roberts, *Dvr*

Adams, *Dvr*

Hughes, *Dvr*

Hudson, *Dvr*

Morgan, *Dvr*

Perrins, *Dvr*

Pole, *Dvr*

Sidwell, *Dvr*

Symonds, *Dvr*

Slatham, *Dvr*

Thompson, *Dvr*

West, *Dvr*

Barnitt, *Dvr*

Williams, *Dvr*

ATTACHED PERSONNEL

Jones, *Sgt Major (Medic)*

Seeney, *Pte (Medic)*

Bex, *Pte (Medic)*

Beasley, *Dvr (Army Service Corps)*

South, *Dvr (Army Service Corps)*

ATTACHED PERSONNEL (Cont.)

Gate, *Dvr (Army Service Corps)*

Taylor, *Dvr (Army Service Corps)*

Smith, *Dvr (Army Service Corps)*

Weighall, *Dvr (Army Service Corps)*

Withers, *Dvr (Army Service Corps)*

Smith, *Dvr (Army Service Corps)*

Appendix B

1/1 WARWICKSHIRE RHA
ROLL OF WAR DEAD

Alford S, *Bdr*

Bailey AW, *Gnr*

Bain D, *Gnr*

Bex G, *Pte*

Brown J, *Gnr*

Bull TH, *Gnr*

Caldicott FW, *Gnr*

Collingbourne HC, *Gnr*

Coomes JS, *Gnr*

Cope FO, *A/Bdr*

Crowther GF, *Bdr*

Dearling EJ, *Gnr*

De Heriz, *Gnr*

Dicks CH, *Gnr*

Duckworth PB, *2nd Lieut*

Durran JF, *Wheeler*

Eaton F, *Bdr*

Edmunds GE, *Cpl*

Evans J, *Dvr*

Facer HA, *Gnr*

Fitzgerald P, *Gnr*

Gerrish W, *Bdr*

Glover L, *Lieut*

Goodman AF, *Gnr*

Hill JT, *Bdr*

Hotchin JG, *Cpl*

Hughes IN, *Gnr*

Jackson P, *A/Cpl*

Jones F, *Gnr*

Kay NR, *Lieut*

Keen F, *Cpl*

Kinman N, *Sgt (MM)*

Lane-Mullins JB, *2nd Lieut*

LeFeaux JF, *2nd Lieut*

Nicholls G, *Gnr*

Nichols GA, *2nd Lieut*

Nichols WH, *Bdr*

North HA, *Gnr*

Peterkins J, *Gnr*

Phillips E, *A/Bdr*

Priest WA, *Dvr*

Reeve EF, *Gnr*

Robinson RE, *Gnr*

Rollason HE, *Bdr*

Sadler A, *Bdr*

Salter JE, *Gnr*

Sharland RM, *Cpl*

Smith AB, *BQMS*

Swan, *Lieut*

Taylor BF, *Bdr*

The Earl Poulett, *Capt*

Walsh JH, *Dvr*

Wheeler AFL, *Gnr*

Wilday F, *Gnr*

Williams O, *Bdr*

Williams EJ, *Gnr*

Winyard H, *S/Sgt*

Wood B, *Dvr*

Woodhouse KC, *Lieut*

Worral F, *Gnr*

Appendix C

SKETCH MAP OF WARWICKSHIRE (PRE-1974)

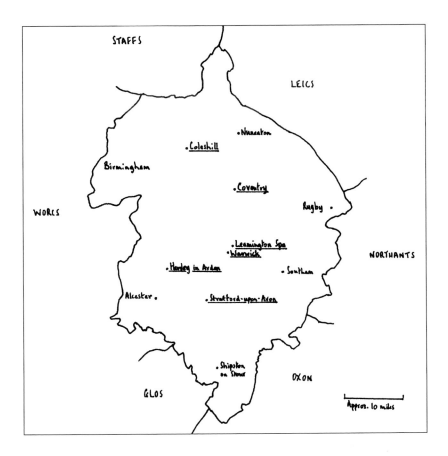

The towns which provided the sub-sections of 1/1 Warwickshire RHA are underlined.

Appendix D

1/1 WARWICKSHIRE RHA
AWARDS AND DECORATIONS
(1914-1918)

Ackerman AV, *Sergeant*	Mention in Dispatches
Ashley P, *Driver*	Military Medal
Bishop J, *Driver*	Card of Honour
Bull C, *A/BSM*	Military Medal; French Croix de Guerre
Checkley E, *Sergeant*	Mention in Dispatches
Collingridge A, *Sergeant*	Military Medal
Dixon GHS, *Lieutenant*	Military Cross
Dixon HJ, *Gunner*	Military Medal
Eden RE, *Major*	Military Cross; Mention in Dispatches
Franklin FW, *Sergeant*	Meritorious Service Medal
Hayes F, *BQMS*	Meritorious Service Medal
Keen GHM, *Corporal*	Military Medal
Kinman WN, *Sergeant*	Military Medal and Bar
Malby HF, *2nd Lieutenant*	Military Cross
Marks JH, *Bombardier*	Card of Honour
Mure GRG, *Captain*	Military Cross; Mention in Dispatches (2); Belgian Ordre de la Couronne and Croix de Guerre

Murray WA, *Major*	Distinguished Service Order and Mention in Dispatches
Perks JC, *Gunner*	Military Medal
Perrins LG, *Bombardier*	Military Medal
Peto RA, *Lieutenant*	Mention in Dispatches
Philip RT, *2nd Lieutenant*	Military Cross
Poole LR, *Gunner*	Military Medal
Roxburgh WE, *Sergeant*	Military Medal
Shirley G, *S/Sergeant Farrier*	Meritorious Service Medal
Smith AG, *Sergeant*	Mention in Dispatches
Stone HS, *Driver*	Military Medal
Thomason B, *Bombardier*	Military Medal

(Ranks are as when the awards were earned.)

Appendix E

1/1 WARWICKSHIRE RHA
BATTERY COMMANDERS

1908–1913   Lord Brooke
1913–1916   Major WAS Gemmell
1916–1917   Major WA Murray
1917–1919   Major RE Eden